THE BRADSHAW GARDENING GUIDES

Get up to date on the most important developments in gardening technology — the newest machines, chemicals, seeds, gardening aids and methods — and profit from John Bradshaw's many years of experience at the same time. This all-new series is the definitive guide to the what, why, where and how of successful modern gardening in 16 fully illustrated volumes.

- The Lawn Book
- Growing Gourmet Vegetables
- Annual Flowers
- The Indoor Plant Primer
- The Complete Book of Bulbs
- Evergreens
- Perennial Flowers
- A Guide to the Balcony Garden
- The Shrubbery Book
- Growing Garden Fruit
- Roses
- A Guide to Children's Gardens
- Biennials for the Specialty Garden
- The Book of Trees
- The Landscaping Manual
- Controlling Garden Pests

John Bradshaw

Growing Gourmet Vegetables

How to Eat
the Best for Less

MALAK

McClelland and Stewart

McClelland and Stewart Limited
The Canadian Publishers
25 Hollinger Road
Toronto, Ontario
M4B 3G2

Canadian Cataloguing in Publication Data

Bradshaw, John, 1916-
  Growing gourmet vegetables

(Bradshaw gardening guides; 2)
ISBN 0-7710-1553-4

1. Vegetable gardening.
I. Title. II. Series: Bradshaw, John, 1916-
Bradshaw gardening guides; 2.

SB321.B72   635   C82-094832-2

Design and Illustrations: Pamela Patrick/Anodos Studios
Design Concept: R.K. Studios
Cover Photo: Northrup King & Co., Minneapolis, Minnesota
Author Photo: Nir Bareket
Special thanks to John F. Gale, President, Stokes Seeds Limited,
St. Catharines, Ontario

Printed and Bound in United States of America.

TEN BASIC RULES
FOR SUCCESSFUL GARDENING

1. Use the right tools for the job and keep them well-maintained.

2. Know your soil and condition it with the proper humus and fertilizer.

3. Plan your gardens and grounds well in advance of sowing or planting.

4. Choose the seed to suit your needs and your growing season.

5. Know your local frost dates and adjust your planting schedule to suit your climate.

6. Learn to recognize when and how much to water.

7. Cultivate to keep roots healthy and weeds in check.

8. Make sure the light conditions are right.

9. Know your enemies and eliminate pests or diseases as soon as they appear.

10. Use pesticides, fertilizers and other chemicals sparingly and carefully.

Contents

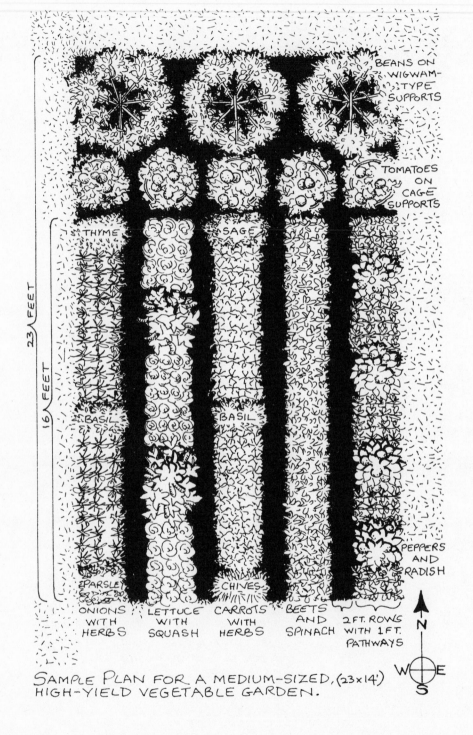

BEANS ON WIGWAM-TYPE SUPPORTS

TOMATOES ON CAGE SUPPORTS

23 FEET

16 FEET

THYME

SAGE

BASIL

BASIL

PEPPERS AND RADISH

PARSLEY

CHIVES

ONIONS WITH HERBS

LETTUCE WITH SQUASH

CARROTS WITH HERBS

BEETS AND SPINACH

2 FT. ROWS WITH 1 FT. PATHWAYS

N
W E
S

SAMPLE PLAN FOR A MEDIUM-SIZED, (23x14')
HIGH-YIELD VEGETABLE GARDEN.

Introduction

In recent years, millions of North Americans have rediscovered the joy of growing vegetables and eating them fresh from the garden. The latest statistics show that over 50 million home gardeners in the United States and Canada are harvesting some 18 billion dollars' worth of produce each year!

The home vegetable garden offers a wonderfully relaxing, healthy and profitable hobby to city and country dwellers alike. People of all ages are deriving tremendous satisfaction from eating the vegetables they've grown in their own backyards. Children in particular are fascinated to watch the plants grow and delighted to have their "very own" garden.

Before the resurgence of vegetable gardening in the 1960's, most varieties were bred so that they could be mechanically harvested in California, Florida or Mexico and still arrive at far-away fruit and vegetable counters looking fresh. This meant that the breeder's primary interest was durability and a great deal of fibre was therefore bred into the vegetables at the expense of quality and flavor. We now have varieties which I call "gourmet", a term the dictionary defines as table delicacies. And there's certainly no doubt that garden-fresh vegetables are cheaper, more nutritious and better tasting.

The Gallup Poll of Gardening indicates that some 7 million people are now growing vegetables in containers, both outdoors and indoors. To keep up with this trend, breeders are creating new dwarf, bush varieties of tomato, cucumber, squash and eggplant which are ideal for cultivation in a small garden. Indoors, given a sunny window or a special light set-up, you can grow many delectable vegetables and herbs, some of them even during the winter months.

If you're thinking of growing your own vegetables, it's a good idea to invest in a large freezer. You can then enjoy them at their delicious best, fresh from the garden, and continue to have the highest quality frozen produce throughout the year. **It's important to take into consideration your freezing or storage capacity when planning the size of your garden and in determining how much of any particular vegetable to grow.**

The Vegetable Garden

Planning Your Garden

Gardening on paper during the winter months is not only fun, it's essential. Ordering your seeds early is important, particularly with new varieties where the supply may be limited for the first year. If you wish to start some seeds indoors yourself or have them grown by a nursery, then the earlier you get your order in the better. The time to start planning your garden is when the seed catalogues arrive in late December or early January. You may have your eye on some uncommon variety and by letting your local supplier know of your requirements well in advance he may be able to obtain the seeds for you along with his normal order. Unless you're starting all your own plants, it will pay to find a small local grower for your special requirements. The large nurseries and garden outlets usually stock only the most popular varieties.

One of the best guides to planning a vegetable garden is a seed catalogue from a reliable firm. So it's a good idea to make sure you're on the mailing list of several companies. The better catalogues are made to be as informative as possible. For example, let's say you're interested in snap beans. For each variety, you should find good color photographs and a detailed description which includes the number of days it will take from the time the seed is sown until the first beans are ready for eating. The catalogue should also give basic directions for cultivating and growing the beans and the length of row each package will sow. There is a wealth of information in seed catalogues which can be a real help in mapping out your vegetable garden. **For a list of recommended seed firms, see page** 97.

At this stage, it's a good practice to take a large piece of paper or cardboard and sketch in the number of rows and the number of plants in each row to a rough scale. An important point to keep in mind is that early crops should be located either on the right or left side of the garden. **The entire plan must be reversed each year so that you aren't growing the same vegetable in one spot 2 years in succession.**

Remember also that if you arrange your vegetable garden so that the rows run north and south, the plants will get the maximum amount of sun. Light is vitally important and every part of the garden should receive a minimum of 5 hours of full sunshine daily. Where large trees

MALAK

11

may shade the garden, enough sun can often be obtained by removing their lower limbs.

Choosing Your Seed, All-America Selections

One of the most important non-profit gardening organizations in the United States and Canada is All-America Selections Incorporated. It was established in 1932 for the purpose of pre-introductory testing, rating and screening of proposed new varieties of vegetables, flowers and roses from seed breeders around the world. Those that win a coveted All-America award represent the finest and most noteworthy new breeds in each category.

Amateur gardeners as well as professional and commercial plant breeders from all over the world send their most promising new creations for entry into the trials. Here, carefully selected judges evaluate them on the basis of their behavior in each of the trial locations.

For award points and recommendation by a judge, the new variety must show distinctiveness, usefulness and desirability. It must be superior to others of its kind and purpose, given the soil and climatic conditions of the trial location. Total award points from all the flower and vegetable judges will determine which entries are to be considered for bronze, silver or gold medals and which will be introduced as "All-America Selections".

Look for the special A.A.S. emblem or certification mark in the seed catalogue or at seed displays to discover superior varieties and garden delights.

Fleuroselect is the European equivalent to A.A.S. and their winners are treated with the same respect as the All-America Selections.

Location and Size

It's difficult to recommend a definite size for the garden because it will depend almost entirely on its location. For example, the ideal location for a small, city garden would be a sunny area measuring 10ft x 10ft (3m x 3m), or part of the flower border that's approximately 5ft (1.5m) wide and 20ft (6m) long. In this type of garden, it's advisable to grow a succession of quick-maturing vegetables that can be planted close together. These would include radishes, lettuce, green onions, beets, carrots, spinach, snap beans, and 5 or 6 tomato plants, grown on stakes or in containers.

Home gardeners with enough space for a larger garden, and who intend to grow most of their own vegetables for year-round use, will need a plot at least 1,500sq ft (135sq m) in area, say 30ft (9m) long by 50ft (15m) wide.

In many North American cities it's now possible to rent a plot of land in a community garden which is either run commercially or made available by the municipality. The gardening poll has shown that the average dollar savings per garden is high enough to make even the rental of a community garden very worthwhile. These gardens are usually watered, plowed, and manured before you take over in the early spring.

Conditioning the Soil

The success of your vegetable garden depends a great deal on the soil being well-drained. An area where the water collects and stays for a long time, in the spring or after heavy summer rains, should not be used for this purpose. A reliable indicator of poor drainage is the formation of a green scum on the surface of the soil or the presence of many cracks after the earth has finally dried out. If you have this problem you may be able to correct it by laying drainage tile which will carry the water away.

There's no doubt that a sandy loam soil containing plenty of humus is ideal for growing vegetables. Unfortunately, all too many home gardeners have to contend with soils that are not nearly as serviceable as sandy loam. The good news is that almost any soil can be conditioned to grow vegetables. Both the very light sandy soils and the heavy clays can be improved by digging in large quantities of humus in the spring, just as soon as the earth becomes workable, and again in the fall before the garden is put to bed for the winter.

Humus

Which humus you use will depend almost entirely upon price and availability. Material from the home garden compost factory is by far the cheapest and the best. Composted cattle manure, spent mushroom manure, composted horse or poultry manure (at least one year old), or peat moss are all satisfactory for vegetable gardening. If you have reasonably good top soil, use 10 bushels (352L) for each 100sq ft (9sq m). In those gardens where the earth is more like subsoil, 15 bushels (529L) per 100sq ft (9sq m) will not be too much.

For gardening on a large or small scale, then, a home compost factory is a must. Here you can turn any leafy material into valuable humus at almost no cost.

I should note here that, contrary to popular opinion, no undesirable odors will be generated by your compost box and it won't attract vermin such as rats and mice. The process is a completely clean one.

Making Humus

Building a home compost factory is neither difficult nor expensive. For the average garden, a box 6ft (1.8m) long by 4ft (1.2m) wide, and 4 to 6ft (1.2 to 1.8m) deep would be sufficient — it won't require a bottom or a top. Some people with very large gardens like to have 2 boxes side by side.

The container can be made of any rough lumber that's available and a visit to the wrecker may be worthwhile in this regard. Plaster laths, snow fencing or concrete blocks can also be used, but most people make the box out of wood. If you follow this method, it's wise to paint the boards inside and out with copper waterproofing paint. This will help prevent the lumber from rotting too quickly and will considerably prolong the life of your compost factory. The outside of the box can be coated with a second layer of outdoor paint to match the house or garage.

If you start adding material to the box in early spring, you'll have a substantial supply of excellent humus by fall. It is possible, however, to make usable compost in 3 to 4 weeks if you can't wait the normal 4 to 6 months. A special cutting blade which fits any rotary mower and which finely grinds all the leafy materials has recently been introduced to the marketplace. The resulting mixture is placed in special plastic bags with air cells that permit the material to breathe. I've made satisfactory compost in a week using this new method.

A heat build-up in the center of the compost pile is all-important to quick composting. If you're adding grass clippings, cabbage leaves or similar green material, you should mix some tougher material with it, such as weeds, straw or dry leaves. The best plan is to pregrind any of the trash material so that the particles are about 1in. (2.5cm) in diameter, maximum. This will ensure that the temperature in the center of the box will quickly reach the level which encourages the hard-working bacteria to flourish.

A compost factory that's too shallow will not do the job because there won't be enough compacted trash to create this heat build-up. Researchers have found that 4 to 6ft (1.2 to 1.8m) is the optimum height to insulate the material and prevent heat loss. As the trash is converted to humus, the pile will shrink to about 3ft (1m).

The trash material must be kept moist at all times, but not so wet that oxygen is prevented from circulating. Green refuse such as cabbage and lettuce leaves need no water at all in the beginning, but dry leaves, stalks and grass clippings should be dampened as they are added to the pile. The moisture contained in the entire pile should be no more than you could squeeze out of the average sponge.

For quick composting, the material should be turned every 3 or 4 days. This will aerate the compost, give you a chance to adjust the moisture level, and allow the bacteria access to trash that was on the outside of the pile. If you're not interested in speeding up the natural process, turning the material once a month will be sufficient.

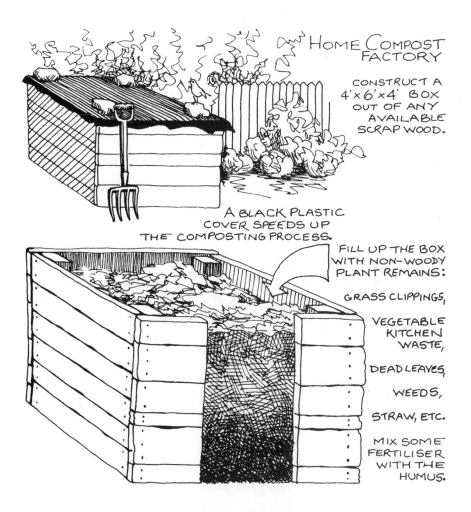

HOME COMPOST FACTORY

CONSTRUCT A 4'x6'x4' BOX OUT OF ANY AVAILABLE SCRAP WOOD.

A BLACK PLASTIC COVER SPEEDS UP THE COMPOSTING PROCESS.

FILL UP THE BOX WITH NON-WOODY PLANT REMAINS:

GRASS CLIPPINGS,

VEGETABLE KITCHEN WASTE,

DEAD LEAVES,

WEEDS,

STRAW, ETC.

MIX SOME FERTILISER WITH THE HUMUS.

Faster and better composting can also be achieved by covering the compost factory with black plastic. This greatly increases the heat build-up in the center of the pile by attracting the sun and helping to retain its warmth.

Start your home garden compost by adding material and tamping it down until you have a layer about 6in (15cm) deep. Adjust the moisture level and then cover this first layer with 1in (2.5cm) of top soil to improve the texture of the humus. Start a second layer on top and continue in this manner until the compost box is filled.

Not only will your vegetable garden require large quantities of humus, it will need plant food as well. The best way to ensure a good supply is to combine the humus with a complete garden fertilizer, such as a 4-12-8 or a 5-10-5, at the rate of 4lbs (1.8kg) per 100sq ft (9sq m).

For the small garden, say 10ft x 10ft (3m x 3m), the best method is to spade the humus and fertilizer into the soil. For the larger garden, you'll probably want to use rotary tillage equipment. Stay away from the light hand-drawn models; they're never able to do the job. Excellent motorized tillers are widely available, either to buy or rent. Over 50 per cent of home gardeners now prepare their vegetable gardens using one of these machines.

Very often with a new home the lot is full of weeds, lacking in humus and in need of considerable effort (and money) before a satisfactory lawn may be created. In such cases, given the expense already involved in starting a new home, the best thing to do is to work humus and a complete garden fertilizer into the soil, as outlined earlier. Then plant a garden using potatoes, tomatoes and any other vegetables that require considerable hoeing. Potatoes do a particularly fine job of getting the soil in shape for seeding or sodding a lawn and, at the same time, provide some good eating.

If the crop is put in early, you can start digging potatoes at the beginning of July and they'll be out of the way by mid-August. This works out well because the best time for sowing or sodding the new lawn is the last week of August or the first 3 weeks in September. Carrying out this plan is even easier now that potatoes can be grown from seed and treated like other bedding plants.

There's one important way of improving the soil each year which should always be a part of good vegetable gardening practice. Around the middle of August, when the early vegetables are finished, work humus and a complete garden fertilizer into the soil, as recommended earlier. Then sow a fall crop of rye grass. Seed is widely available from garden outlets, nurseries and mail order catalogues. This will produce what is called a green manure crop which will be several inches (8-10cm) high by the time the growing season ends in late fall. It will live over the winter and can be turned under early in May when it will be about 18in (45cm) high. Such green manure crops are perfect for building up the supply of humus in the soil and in 2 or 3 years you will be very close to having a first-class garden loam.

Cultivation

Frequent cultivation is essential when growing vegetables. Weeds must be destroyed as soon as they appear or they'll rob the vegetable plants of precious food and moisture. Cultivation just as soon as the soil surface has dried after a rain or watering from the hose will also prevent the earth from forming a hard crust and give the air a chance to circulate oxygen through the earth and to the roots. In most tem-

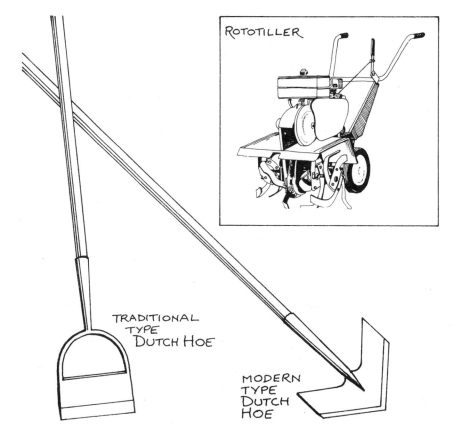

ROTOTILLER

TRADITIONAL
TYPE
DUTCH HOE

MODERN
TYPE
DUTCH
HOE

perate areas, the first weeds begin to show up around the middle of May.

Be sure to cultivate shallowly at all times, but be particularly careful after the middle of June when the vegetable plants will have developed a root system close to the surface of the earth.

Chemicals are not recommended for weed control in the home garden. These selective weed killers are widely used by commercial vegetable growers who plant many acres with one vegetable. But a chemical that's safe and effective for one type of plant can severely injure or kill another one close by.

In all but the largest vegetable gardens, it's best to cultivate the space between the rows by hand. For most people it's a pleasant and rewarding form of exercise. For this purpose, you'll need a Dutch hoe which consists of a sharp blade on a long handle. Such a hoe will enable you to cultivate backwards, pushing instead of pulling, thus eliminating any shoe marks. You will also be able to cultivate as shallowly as needed, much better than with the conventional hoe.

Mulching

Covering the surface of the earth between the plants with humus or plastic will cut down on the amount of cultivation needed, keep the earth cooler, and help conserve soil moisture. I recommend cultivating freely until June 20 and then applying a mulch of plastic or humus 3 to 4in (7.5 to 10cm) deep. Straw, grass clippings and any of the forms of humus used to prepare the soil for growing vegetables all make satisfactory mulches.

Early-maturing vegetables such as lettuce, radishes, spinach, early cabbage, and potatoes won't benefit from mulching because they'll be harvested before the mulch has had sufficient time to be effective.

Watering

To grow top-quality vegetables which yield well and have good flavor, the earth must contain a uniform and adequate supply of moisture at all times. From the 1st of June onwards rainfall is usually inadequate and the home gardener must be prepared to give the vegetable garden a good soaking once a week. **Avoid daily light sprinklings which merely encourage surface rooting and provide little or no benefit to the plants.**

Early in the season the roots will be close to the surface and the water needs to penetrate the earth to a maximum depth of 6in (15cm). This will be sufficient throughout June and July, but starting in early August the water must penetrate 8 to 10in (20 to 25cm) into the earth. This means leaving the sprinkler in one spot for 2 hours or more for each watering during August.

One of the best ways of applying the water is to lay a plastic soaker hose between the rows and let it gradually release water at a rate that can be absorbed by the soil. It's a serious mistake to stand with a hose and try to water the vegetable garden. Many newcomers to gardening don't realize that if water is sprinkled onto the soil too fast the surface will become supersaturated. When this occurs, very little additional water can penetrate the soil and the excess just runs off to the nearest drain and is wasted.

Feeding

A complete garden fertilizer will contain balanced amounts of 3 major ingredients — nitrogen, phosphorus and potash — plus valuable trace elements such as magnesium and iron. Nitrogen stimulates the green growth of the plants, phosphorus aids in root growth and enhances the color of flowers, fruits and vegetables, while potash promotes the overall health of trees and plants in much the same way as vitamins do in animals.

In addition to adding a quantity of complete garden fertilizer to the soil before seeding or setting out transplants, further feedings will be needed once a month during the growing season. The number of times you feed them will depend on how long it takes for the particular vegetable to reach maturity. Radishes require only one feeding before harvesting, snap beans and peas two feedings, squashes and turnips as many as three. For very small gardens, a soluable, complete garden fertilizer is probably the easiest to handle. In large gardens, scatter 2in (5cm) of a dry, complete garden fertilizer on either side of each row, then take a Dutch hoe or garden rake and gently work the fertilizer into the surface of the soil. Where a mulch has already been put in place, the fertilizer can be scattered on top and then watered in. With plastic mulches the material can be lifted up and the fertilizer scattered along the surface of the earth, worked in with a Dutch hoe or garden rake, and the plastic replaced.

A Late Vegetable Garden

In early July you can begin an important fall garden using either seeds or started plants. The following vegetables are excellent for this purpose:

Cauliflower

Brussel Sprouts

Cabbage

Kale

Beets

Carrots

Lettuce

Turnips

Swiss Chard

Zucchini

Snap Beans

No special care is required. The earth should be prepared in exactly the same way as for the spring garden and the various vegetables given similar treatment. Cauliflower, cabbage and Brussel sprouts should be started from seed sown outdoors in the beginning of June and then transplanted into the vegetable garden. Once they're set in, give each one a cupful of special starter solution to overcome transplanting shock and to get them off to a fast start.

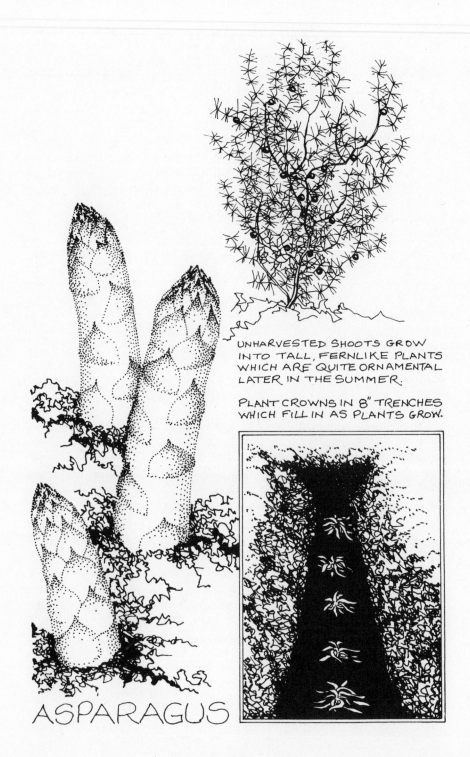

UNHARVESTED SHOOTS GROW
INTO TALL, FERNLIKE PLANTS
WHICH ARE QUITE ORNAMENTAL
LATER IN THE SUMMER.

PLANT CROWNS IN 8" TRENCHES
WHICH FILL IN AS PLANTS GROW.

ASPARAGUS

Asparagus

Nearly all the vegetables we grow in the garden are annuals or are treated as such. The major exception to this rule is the delectable asparagus, which comes to our North American gardens from Europe, Asia and North Africa.

Since an asparagus bed will last anywhere from 10 to 15 years or more, it's rarely planted in the small garden and is better suited to the suburban or country garden. Three years after planting, the first crop can be harvested but it will be 5 years before the bed is in full production.

Preparation, Planting and Care

The home gardener must realize that the performance of this truly gourmet vegetable will be in direct proportion to how carefully and how well the planting bed is prepared. In this regard, keep in mind that the asparagus is a deep-rooted vegetable which requires very fertile soil containing plenty of humus. Sandy loams are by far the best but you can add extra large amounts of humus and fertilizer to a very light sandy soil and still get good results. I don't believe there's any point in trying to grow asparagus in a heavy clay that's poorly drained.

It's absolutely essential that the earth in which you plan to grow asparagus is completely free of perennial weeds and grasses such as twitch, otherwise known as quackgrass or couch.

Because the asparagus plants are going to completely occupy the soil for such a long period of time, the preparation before planting must be extremely thorough. I would recommend beginning the year before you plan to put the asparagus plants in the ground, but it's not absolutely essential. You'll need plenty of humus, say 15 bushels (529L) per 100sq ft (9sq m) of bed area, to dig into the earth. The following types of humus may be used for asparagus: composted cattle manure, spent mushroom manure, material from the home garden compost factory, or composted horse or poultry manure that's at least one year old. You'll also need about 4lbs (1.8kg) per 100sq ft (9sq m) of a complete garden fertilizer such as a 4-12-8 or a 5-10-5. The humus and fertilizer should be worked into the earth using a spade or rotary tiller down to a minimum depth of 10in (25cm).

Plants already flourishing in containers are considered to be the best for transplanting to the garden. If you are forced to buy bare-root plants, be sure to discard any with very small crowns and all damaged or withered plants. Bare-root plants must be kept under a piece of moistened burlap or in a bucket partially filled with water to prevent injury from wind or sun.

Asparagus roots are widely available from nurseries, garden outlets and mail order seed catalogues. You can also easily grow your own plants from seed. While asparagus plants are perfectly hardy and produce their delectable spears in the spring, the seed won't germinate well in cool weather. This means you'll need to sow indoors in March or April, and no earlier than the 1st of June (after the soil and air temperature has completely warmed up) if you sow outdoors. Germination will occur much more readily if you first soak the seeds for 48 hours in water heated to 100°F (38°C).

Seeds can be sown in peat fibre, plastic or clay pots, or in drills out in the garden. In either case, they should be covered with ½in (1cm) of soil and will germinate in 2 or 3 weeks. Space the seeds sown outdoors 5in (12.5cm) apart and, when the seedlings are 2in (5cm) high, thin to one strong plant every 18in (45cm). In early September, those growing in containers may be transplanted to their permanent bed in the garden.

Planting early in the spring is recommended. After preparing the soil as described above, remove any debris and dig a furrow 8in (20cm) deep. It should be wide enough to allow the roots to spread out on all sides without crowding. Next, lightly but evenly dust the bottom of the furrow with a complete garden fertilizer. To prevent the roots from coming into direct contact with the fertilizer and being burnt, finish off with a 1in (2.5cm) layer of soil. This preliminary feeding is essential; after the crop is established, such deep placement of the required phosphorus and potash will not be possible.

The crowns should be set in the furrow, 6 to 7in (15 to 17.5cm) deep and spaced 18in (45cm) apart. In the beginning, they should be covered with just 2in (5cm) of well-firmed soil. As the new plants grow taller, the furrow will gradually become full. Rows of asparagus are spaced 4ft (1.2m) apart.

After planting, the asparagus must be cultivated regularly every season to keep weeds and grasses in check. In the first and second seasons, spray or dust the plants every 2 weeks to keep insects like the asparagus beetle under strict control. During the third season, when you start picking, delay using insecticides until the harvest is over. Every fall the tops of the plants will turn brown but they should not be removed until early in the following spring.

The first spring after planting, and for each successive year, apply a complete garden fertilizer at the rate of 4lbs (1.8kg) per 100sq ft (9sq m)

Rust-resistant Viking is an outstanding strain of asparagus.

STOKES SEEDS LTD.

of bed area. Work it lightly into the soil just as soon as the earth has thawed.

Many people are unable to stop themselves from cutting the spears (the edible tops of the plants) in their second year of growth. This is extremely harmful as it inhibits the development of an adequate root system. I'm happy to say though that, if you simply don't have enough will-power, cutting over a period of a week to 10 days maximum doesn't appear to do much harm.

When cutting asparagus, choose spears that are 6 or 7in (15 to 17.5cm) long and use a sharp knife. The cut should be made 1 to 1-1/2in (2.5 to 4cm) below the surface of the earth. Be careful not to injure any young spears that are developing nearby. Bear in mind also that the longer the spear, the more bitter the taste.

Asparagus spears lose their good eating quality soon after they've been picked if they're kept warm and dry, so cook or freeze them immediately. If you do want them to last for a few days, keep them in the refrigerator or some other cool place with the bunches of spears set on end in a shallow pan of water.

Gourmet Asparagus
- **Waltham Washington** — A superior, high-yielding variety, producing up to 30 per cent more stalks than other asparagus.
- **Mary Washington V35/Vineland/Viking** — An outstanding strain, highly resistant to rust.
- **Faribo Hybrid** — An excellent, rust-resistant cross, producing the largest, heaviest stalks and thus increasing total yields by 30 per cent.

Beans

Snap beans and tomatoes are the two most popular and widely grown vegetables in North America. At one time, snap beans were known as string beans but since our plant breeders have eliminated the fibre and strings in the gourmet varieties the name no longer applies. Why are they called "snap" beans? Take a pod of green or yellow beans, break it with your fingers and see how it snaps.

I find that snap beans are a wonderful way to get children interested in gardening. Youngsters need quick results and seeds or plants that are large enough for them to handle. Snap beans qualify in both respects; the seeds are large and they germinate very quickly. After the soil temperature reaches 60°F (16°C) or higher, the seedlings will pop through the ground as soon as a week after sowing.

Preparation, Planting and Care

All beans are members of the legume family. They have nodules attached to their roots that enable them to take the free nitrogen from the air and use it to feed themselves. You can give this process a real boost by treating the seed with a commercial legume innoculant so that more nodules will form. These innoculants are widely available in the form of a black powder. You can either soak the seeds in water and then dip them in the powder, or simply dust it along the seeding furrow just before you sow.

For snap beans to grow well, the earth must contain a plentiful supply of humus and fertilizer. Whatever fertilizer you choose for beans should be low in nitrogen but contain fairly high amounts of phosphorus and potash, such as a 4-12-8 or a 5-10-5. Keep in mind the nitrogen-fixing ability of the beans and the fact that if the fertilizer contains a lot of nitrogen, very few pods will be produced and the plant growth will be soft and mushy.

Apply the fertilizer to the soil at a rate of 4lbs (1.8kg) per 100sq ft (9sq m) of row area, or follow the manufacturer's directions. Don't go by the theory that, if a little will do some good, a lot will be even better. Adding "one for the pot" may make a better cup of coffee, but it never works that way with chemicals in your garden.

Humus should be scattered on top of the fertilizer at the rate of 10 bushels (352L) per 100sq ft (9sq m) of row area. Mix the earth, humus and fertilizer together thoroughly down to a depth of 8in (20cm). Rake level and remove any debris, then use the end of the rake or garden hoe to make a furrow 1-1/2in (4cm) deep.

Space your rows 18in (45cm) apart and space the seeds 3in (7.5cm) apart. Before sowing, fill the furrow with water and allow it to drain away, then scatter the legume innoculant. The seeds should be covered with fine soil, firmed gently with your foot or the back of a hoe or rake.

Under good growing conditions, the beans will be up in a week. When the plants are 2 to 3in (5 to 7.5cm) high, thin them to 5in (13cm) apart.

For a continuous supply of beans, make a sowing every 2 weeks from the time the temperature of the soil reaches 60°F (16°C), usually sometime in May, until the first week of August. If your climate permits, you can plant even later. A plastic greenhouse structure placed over the beans can protect them from early frosts in cooler regions and allow for an extra late sowing.

At 5 or 6in (13 or 15cm) high, the plants are ready for a second feeding with the complete garden fertilizer. Scatter the plant food along both sides of the row and work it gently into the surface of the earth with a rake or Dutch hoe.

Beginning in June, give the plants a good soaking with the hose once a week, unless there's been adequate rainfall. The sprinkler should be left in one spot for 2 hours to allow the moisture to penetrate the earth down to a depth of at least 6in (15cm).

Gourmet Snap Beans

You must be very careful in your choice of varieties for the garden. Avoid those like Spartan Arrow, Harvester or Provider which are favorites of the commercial grower. They've been bred to have their beans mature all at once to allow for mechanical harvesting. You'll usually find the phrase "concentrated set" in the variety description. Choose those that are specially listed for home garden use and they will yield over an extended period.

- **Contender and Bountiful** — Two varieties which can withstand cold, damp soil conditions and thus allow a 10 day jump on the bean season. They're free of fibre and excel in tenderness and flavor.
- **Top Crop** — The most flavorful main crop bean whether fresh, frozen or canned. Alternative varieties are: **Tendergreen, Tendercrop, Greensleeves, and Tenderette.**
- **Roma** — The bush form of the famous *Pole romano* starts early in the season and needs no support.
- **Royalty** — A prolific snap bean with two distinctive characteristics: it has a built-in blanch indicator to aid in freezing (the color turns from purple to deep green); and the seeds will germinate in colder soils than all other beans except Topcrop and Bountiful.

The distinctive purple snap bean, Royalty.

Yellow snap beans, the favorite for freezing.

Gourmet Yellow Snap Beans

Yellow snapgreens are the favorite for freezing. The best are:

- **Pencil Pod Wax** — Meaty pods are borne profusely over a long growing season.
- **Eastern Butterwax** — The hardiest and earliest wax bean, with particularly long, plump and crisp pods.
- **Goldcrop** — An All-America winner, bred for resistance to disease and to produce pods high on the bushes for easy picking.

Pole Beans

Pole beans don't bear as early as snap beans, but make up for this in heavier yields over a longer growing period. The 5 to 8ft (1.5 to 2.4m) vines must be supported, usually by poles tied together in wigwam

English broadbeans are hardy and flavorful.

Pole beans provide the heaviest yields.

fashion. Supports should be placed about 4ft (1.2m) apart, with several plants growing around each one. Alternatively, the plants may be grown in a row, using a fence, trellis or plastic netting for support. Bean towers are also widely available and are extremely effective with vining beans.

- **Kentucky Wonder** — One of the few pole beans which will produce a large crop without support. It can safely be planted in with the corn and is the most popular of all the green-podded pole beans.

Bush Beans

- **Fava or English Broadbean** — A superior bean in both flavor and hardiness. The large beans look like huge limas and are cooked in the same way.

27

Beets

Before they knew any better, North American gardeners allowed beets sown in May to reach full maturity, harvested them in late September or early October, and then stored them into the late fall and winter months. I believe this may be the basis for a strong hatred of beets shared by many people. It's a shame because young beets and their tops are a tasty respite from the usual snap beans, peas, carrots and potatoes. There is nothing I like better than small home-pickled beets, served with cold cuts.

Preparation, Planting and Care

Beets, like carrots or any other root crop, do not like to be planted in heavy soil. However, most soils can be made light enough by the addition of an appropriate amount of humus before sowing. It should be used at the rate of 10 bushels (352L) per 100sq ft (9sq m) of sowing area, generally speaking. But the first step in preparing the soil is to fertilize.

Scatter the garden with a complete lawn fertilizer, low in nitrogen and fairly high in phosphorus and potash, a 4-12-8 or a 5-10-5, at the rate of 4lbs (1.8kg) per 100sq ft (9sq m) of seeding area. Then apply the humus.

Thoroughly mix the earth, fertilizer and humus together down to a depth of 8in (20cm) using a garden spade or rotary tiller. Rake level, remove any debris, and you're ready to sow or transplant.

A little-known fact is that beets are the only root crop that can safely be transplanted. This means that you can have an extra-early crop by sowing your seeds indoors around the middle of March. Using a plastic seedling flat, sow the seeds in a hobby greenhouse or under fluorescent light. In 7 to 10 days the little seedlings will begin to appear. The best variety of beets for this early spring sowing is Ruby Queen, or possibly one of the new miniature beets. You can transplant them to the garden around May 1, laying them out in rows 15in (38cm) apart and leaving 3in (7.5cm) between each plant.

If you use the regular sowing method, the seed should be in the ground just as the trees start to come into leaf, or when the early tulips begin to bloom.

I've never seen a home gardener yet who didn't sow beets too

BURPEE'S GOLDEN BEETS —

VERY TASTY GOLDEN ROOTS THAT DO NOT BLEED LIKE
RED BEETS, AND THE GREENS OF THIS VARIETY ARE
PARTICULARLY GOOD.

thickly. But this can be a blessing in disguise. When the roots are about the diameter of a lead pencil you must start thinning them, and the leaves and roots you pull out will make for one of the most delicious of garden greens.

To ensure a continuous supply of young beets that you can use fresh or freeze, make the first sowing of the season around May 21, a second in mid-June and the last in the first week of July. The latest seeding will provide beets for winter storage. It seems to me, though, that fewer gardeners will be storing them for late fall or winter use since the taste of fresh-frozen beets is far superior to the traditionally stored vegetables.

For the first early spring sowing, place the seed 1in (2.5cm) deep, increasing this to 2in (5cm) deep for the sowings in late May, mid-June and July. Space the rows of beets 12in (30cm) apart.

Thin the plants when they reach 3 to 4in (7.5 to 10cm) in height, leaving the remaining plants 1-1/2 to 2in (4cm to 5cm) apart. After this, alternate plants should be removed before they crowd each other. Of course, you'll be able to eat these thinnings as greens.

STOKES SEEDS LTD.

Little Mini Ball is ideal for the small garden and for pickling.

A month after sowing, a second feeding should be given using the same complete garden fertilizer employed in preparing the soil. Side-dress each row at the rate of 2lbs (900gm) per 50sq ft (4.5sq m) of row.

Gourmet Beets

- **Ruby Queen** — An AAS bronze medal winner and the most popular beet for early sowing. It's round and red-skinned with sweet, tender, deep crimson flesh.
- **Detroit Dark Red, Short Top** — The best of numerous strains of Detroit Dark Red, both as a main crop and for fall use, canning and freezing. The short 3in (7.5cm) tops allow more beets per row.
- **Winter Keeper** — The best variety to sow in the first week of July for fresh beets in the autumn and for winter storage.
- **Burpee's Golden** — The sweet, golden roots develop rapidly and remain perfectly tender when fully grown. They won't bleed like red beets and the tops make delectable greens.

Miniature Beets

As with carrots, there's now a group of miniature gourmet beets averaging only 1in (2.5cm) in diameter. The small size and short tops of both **Badger** and **Little Mini Ball** make them ideal for the small garden and for pickling. They also freeze well.

Broccoli

Over the past 20 years broccoli has become one of the most popular fresh vegetables in North America. Ninety per cent of the broccoli you buy in the market comes from the lush commercial fields of California. Commercially grown broccoli comes closer to home garden quality than almost any other vegetable. Nevertheless, it still pays to grow your own both for eating fresh and freezing — there's a definite improvement in quality.

It may surprise you to know that broccoli is actually a long-season cauliflower. As with other leafy vegetables, broccoli is nutrionally rich, being an excellent source of vitamins A and C.

Nutritionally rich and a gourmet's delight, broccoli is one of the easiest green vegetables to grow.

Preparation, Planting and Care

Few other green vegetables are as easy to grow in the home garden. Soil should be prepared by working in a generous amount of humus and a complete garden fertilizer, such as a 4-12-8 or a 5-10-5. The method is the same for beans, carrots or beets. Avoid planting broccoli where you've grown any other member of the cabbage family, including Brussel sprouts and cauliflower, the year before.

The quality of broccoli is always higher when it is allowed to mature in cool weather. For this reason, we sometimes sow the seed indoors 6 weeks before setting them out in the garden. The best planting time in the spring is 2 weeks ahead of the normal date for the last frost.

Space the plants 24in (60cm) apart in the row and make the rows the same distance from each other. The second sowing is made in early June. When the new seedlings are 5 to 6in (12.5 to 15cm) high they should be thinned to 24in (60cm) apart. Additional plantings can be made using some of the thinnings but be sure and give each plant a cupful of special starter solution to help them recover from transplanting shock. Starting in June soak the plants well, leaving the sprinkler in one place for 2 hours or until the water has penetrated the soil to a depth of 5 to 6in (12.5 to 15cm).

Two insects which may cause broccoli plants trouble are cabbage worms and aphids. They can easily be controlled, however, by spraying the plants with an insecticide containing malathion.

Gourmet Broccoli

- **Green Comet** — The best variety for transplanting, and an All-America winner. Shoots develop early and are continually replaced when cut. Large center heads stay in prime condition for a remarkably long time.
- **Premium Crop Hybrid** — An AAS silver medal winner and my choice for a main crop sown outdoors in early June. The extra large, single heads hold without premature opening until October.

Brussel Sprouts

The tasty Brussel sprout gets its name from the city of Brussels in Belgium, where botanical records show that they were growing as early as the 13th Century.

The numerous little buds, or sprouts, that appear along the main stem, between the ground and the rosette of leaves at the top, mature over quite a lengthy period of time. The lowest sprouts on each plant are the first to mature but if the minor leaves between them are removed the sprouts will continue to develop all the way up the rather thick stem. As with all vegetables, Brussel sprouts from the garden have superior flavor. Just be careful not to overcook them.

When you're preparing Brussel sprouts, drop them into lots of rapidly boiling water. Keep the water at a constant boil and cook uncovered until the sprouts are just tender-crisp. This method will give you the best color, flavor and the highest possible level of nutrients in the cooked vegetable.

Preparation, Planting and Care

In my experience, too many home gardeners plant Brussel sprouts early, setting them in the ground around May 24 and thereby put them at the mercy of summer heat and insects. It is best to treat them like late cabbage, putting started plants into the ground during the first 10 days of July. The home gardener can easily raise his own plants from seed sown in the middle of May, and the resulting plants can be set in the ground at the beginning of July. Many nurseries and garden centers carry a supply of started plants for the early July planting.

Before planting, prepare the ground well, adding the same amount of humus and complete garden fertilizer as you would for carrots or beans. Set the plants 2ft (60cm) apart, in rows 3ft (90cm) apart. After putting the plants in the ground, give each one a cupful of special starter solution that's very high in phosphorus.

Starting a week after planting, soak the Brussel sprouts once a week, leaving the sprinkler in one spot for 2 hours so the earth is moistened to a minimum depth of 6in (15cm).

Around the middle of September, when the lowest sprouts are beginning to achieve eating, or marketable, size, pinch off the new

W. ATLEE BURPEE CO.

The flavor of "snow survivors", such as Jade Cross E Brussel sprouts and all season radishes, is actually improved by frost.

growing tips on the top of each plant. This will force the sprouts on the upper part of the stems to start developing more rapidly, ensuring firm sprouts of a good size from almost the entire length of the stem.

To keep insect pests completely under control, spray or dust the plants every 10 days with an all-purpose insecticide, specially prepared for vegetables.

Gourmet Brussel Sprouts

• **Jade Cross E** — An F1 hybrid from Japan, this is the only variety of Brussel sprout to grow in the home garden. Hybrid vigor makes it both early and husky in growth. The plants are uniform and productive, fairly tall and loaded from top to bottom with medium-sized, firm, well-wrapped sprouts. They are blue-green and have a fine delicate flavor, whether eaten fresh or frozen. Their excellent taste is actually improved by frosts and they can be picked from the garden all through November and right up until Christmas in most years and in most regions.

34

Cabbage

Cabbages are very much like tomatoes, eggplants, and peppers in that they need to be planted in a soil containing plenty of humus and plant food. This particular vegetable has come to us from the coastal areas of Europe.

STOKES SEEDS LTD.

Hybrid Ruby Ball [above] is the best of the red cabbages.

Flavorful Emerald Cross [right] features uniform shape and hybrid vigor.

W. ATLEE BURPEE CO.

Preparation, Planting and Care

Started cabbage plants can go into the ground as soon as the earth becomes workable in the spring. For early setting, plants can be obtained from nurseries and garden outlets. You're better off growing your own if at all possible, though, because you'll be able to obtain the very best varieties from seed.

If you're sowing seeds indoors, you should begin 7 weeks before the earth can be worked in your area. Germination will take anywhere from 10 days to 2 weeks. Because cabbage is a cool weather crop, a first planting should be made as early as possible, followed by a second one in the first week of July if you want a fall crop. Seeds for the July planting should be sown around May 24 so that you have plants ready to go into the ground by the first week of July.

A complete garden fertilizer, such as a 4-12-8 or a 5-10-5, should be mixed with the humus and worked into the earth before planting. Further feedings should be given monthly until the cabbages are mature. They'll need plenty of moisture, so soak them once a week and make sure the water penetrates the earth to a minimum depth of 6in (15cm). Set the plants in full sun, 18in (45cm) apart.

Gourmet Cabbage

- **Earliana/Golden Acre** — One of the first cabbages to mature, it has uniformly small, attractive heads.
- **Emerald Cross** — An AAS winner that combines fine flavor, uniform shape and hybrid vigor. It stands up particularly well in the garden without bursting after reaching maturity.
- **Savoy King** — My personal favorite and another AAS winner, this is a delightfully tender and flavorful variety with hybrid vigor that ensures heavy production.
- **Danish Ballhead** — The most common late cabbage in the home garden, with heads that stand up well without splitting.
- **Ruby Ball** — The best of the red varieties and an All-America winner, this outstanding hybrid is smaller than most red cabbages and holds for at least a month without splitting.

Carrots

Carrots have a long history, beginning in the eastern Mediterranean where they were widely used by Greeks for medicinal purposes, and by the Romans who took them to England during their long occupation of that country. They were commonly used for food in 17th century England and so it was quite natural for them to arrive in Jamestown, Virginia in 1609 with the first colonists.

Carrots are just about the least perishable of all vegetables and those pulled fresh from the garden for immediate cooking have infinitely more flavor than the commercial varieties grown in California or Mexico. Even stored carrots are better tasting than the fresh-looking imports. Garden carrots also freeze well and miniatures in particular come out of the freezer almost as fresh as they went in.

Preparation, Planting and Care

While carrots are easy to grow, keep in mind that with all root crops the part we eat is produced in the soil. For this reason, it is vitally important that the ground is loose and friable. Carrots grow best in light sandy loams where they normally require little thinning. However, by choosing the correct variety and by digging in plenty of humus, carrots can be grown in almost any soil.

Another important reason for making the soil as loose and friable as possible is that the seedling carrots are very delicate and slow growing. This also means that the earth must be cleared of any large lumps of dirt, stones, sticks and other debris or there will be many misshapen roots and a low yield.

Unless your garden soil is very rich, I'd strongly suggest that you dig in humus before seeding using 12 bushels (423L) per 100ft (30m). Material from the home garden compost factory, composted cattle manure, spent mushroom manure and peat moss are all satisfactory for growing carrots.

A complete garden fertilizer, containing fairly high amounts of phosphorus and potash, should be added at the same time as the humus. Potash is an important plant food element in growing carrots and other root crops which store sugars and starches and a larger than average quantity will be required.

To prepare the earth for sowing, first scatter a complete garden fertilizer, such as a 4-12-8, over the ground and then apply the humus. Mix the soil, fertilizer and humus together down to a depth of at least 8in (20cm). Remember, you must do a particularly good job of raking the ground level and removing debris. Since carrots are only seeded 1/2in (1cm) deep, the best way to create the seeding row is to use a pencil or a small piece of wood and create holes for the seed.

Knowledgeable gardeners often mix some fast-sprouting radish seed, such as Cherry Belle, in with the carrots. Not only will this mark the row but it will also give you an early crop of radishes. With a mixture of 80 per cent carrot seed and 20 per cent radish, the latter will have been pulled and eaten long before they can compete with the carrots.

A first sowing can be made just as soon as the earth becomes workable in the spring. Germination time will be 10 to 15 days if the air temperature is 60°F (16°C) or better. A second sowing can then be made when the first batch is up and growing. Most garden varieties take anywhere from 65 to 70 days to reach maturity. Of course, small immature carrots (pulled to thin out the rows) make a truly gourmet dish. For late fall use and winter storage, a final sowing should be made the first week in July.

Carrots should always be sparsely sown. This is important because roots that are overcrowded will grow slowly and be poorly shaped. The young seedlings should be thinned once they reach 3in (7.5cm) in height, followed by a second thinning 3 weeks later. The plants should then stand about 2in (5cm) apart. Firm the earth around the remaining carrots after each thinning.

Since they are relatively shallow-rooted, carrots will need plenty of water, especially if the weather is hot and dry. It's a big mistake to let the upper 6in (15cm) of soil dry out for any length of time; the resulting carrots won't be nearly as large and they won't taste as good. Give them a thorough soaking once a week starting in the middle of May, or whenever warm weather arrives in your region. Leave the sprinkler in one spot for 2 hours, or long enough so the water penetrates the earth to a depth of 6in (15 cm). •

Gourmet Carrots

- **Nantes** — In addition to the incomparable original French Nantes, there are half a dozen modern varieties deeper in color and coreless, with a similar eating quality. All the Nantes are good for freezing, or eating fresh.
- **Touchon** — The best of the Nantes varieties, entirely suitable for the first outdoor sowing. It's tender and free of woody fibre at all stages of growth.

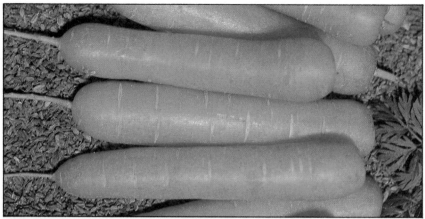

SLUIS & GROOT

Little Finger [above] is coreless and only 2in [5cm] long at maturity.

The miniature Planet [left] is particularly good for freezing.

• **Chantenay** — The most widely grown carrot in home gardens and the best for winter storage or freezing because of its sweetness.

Miniature Carrots

The new miniature carrots from Europe will grow in restricted spaces and mature quickly after sowing. Because their tops are so small, it pays to loosen the earth before pulling the carrots. All miniatures may be frozen without blanching. I would try several varieties to find the one which suits both your individual taste and your garden.

• **Little Finger** — This virtually coreless, early version of the Touchon may be used for canning, pickling, or eating fresh when it reaches 2in (5cm) in length.

• **Sucram** — Originally bred for the gourmet restaurant trade, these 1in (2.5cm) miniatures have the extremely sweet taste of Scarlet Nantes, fresh or frozen.

• **Planet** — This variety is an improved version of Parisienne and is particularly good for freezing. The soil should be hilled up around the plants to prevent green coloration.

CORN

Corn

Many people long for the "good old days", when nearly every family had a huge vegetable garden which supplied not only their daily needs, but produced large quantities of vegetables for canning and storage. But I doubt very much if the home gardener would like to turn the clock back 50 years if he couldn't take modern hybrids with him.

Before the development of hybrids, the most popular varieties of corn were Golden Bantam and Stowell's Evergreen. It is still possible to buy seeds for both, but they can't compare to the modern varieties. Several times over the past few years I've grown Golden Bantam next to a hybrid, and there was absolutely no comparison in flavor, size of cob, or the yield from each plant.

At the turn of the century, all table corn was white; yellow varieties were used only for cattle fodder. With the introduction of Golden Bantam in 1902, table corn gradually became almost exclusively yellow. Recently, the pendulum has begun to swing back toward white corn and probably the only reason yellow corn has survived at all is because of its lateness. Undoubtedly, our breeders will soon develop late white varieties to replace yellow corn completely.

Preparation, Planting and Care

Sweet corn will only grow well in warm soil with good drainage and containing plenty of plant food and humus. It's a proven fact that the soil used to grow corn can hardly ever be too rich.

The ideal time to prepare the earth is immediately before seeding, usually in May. Start by working plenty of humus and a generous amount of garden fertilizer, such as a 4-12-8 or a 5-10-5, into the ground. Mix the earth, fertilizer and humus thoroughly down to a depth of 8in (20cm), using a spade or rotary tiller. Rake level, removing any debris, and you're ready to plant.

Pollination of the corn is vital, and it can be a problem if you must depend on the wind to do the job. One thing you can do to help is to plant several short rows of corn in a block rather than in one long row. This way, when the wind tosses the pollen around, most of the plants will be reached.

You can get a jump on the season by sowing some seeds indoors in pots about 3 weeks before the time your soil would normally reach 60°F (16°C). This is usually in May or the first week in June.

When planting the corn seeds outdoors, always keep in mind that they will rot if put in too soon, when the soil is still cold and wet. Outdoor temperatures should be in the 60-70°F (16-21°C) range and the earth should be moist.

In most areas it's possible to have a long picking season by making 10 successive plantings over the period between May 12 and July 12. Make the rows 3ft (90cm) apart and plant at least 6 rows in a block to ensure pollination. Space the seeds 4 to 6in (10 to 15cm) apart along the row. For the earliest plantings, the seed should be placed only 1/4in (.5cm) under the soil. Later, you can increase the depth to 1in (2.5cm) as the weather gets warmer. Corn seeds usually require 4 to 6 days to germinate at a temperature of 65 to 70°F (18 to 21°C).

Starting in early June, corn will need a good soaking once a week, so that the water penetrates the earth to a depth of 5 to 6in (12.5 to 15cm).

Once the corn plants are 2 to 3in (5 to 7.5cm) high, they'll need to be cultivated frequently to keep the weeds under control. Since most of the roots will be close to the surface, cultivation should be shallow to avoid injury. The best tool for this purpose is the Dutch hoe.

As soon as the plants reach 12in (30cm) in height, it's advisable to hill them up so that they'll be securely anchored in the ground against heavy winds which could blow them over.

Sweet corn must be harvested in what is called the "milk" stage, that is when the kernels exude a thick, milky substance when crushed with the thumbnail. The best stage for picking has passed if the kernel appears doughy or starchy when given the "thumbnail test".

Gourmet Sweet Corn

* **Golden Midget Hybrid and Golden Miniature** — Two miniature varieties which provide the earliest corn and are also excellent for the small garden. Golden Miniature in particular is extremely vigorous, producing an abundance of cobs on dwarf plants.
* **Butterfruit Hybrid** — One of the tastiest and most tender of the new types of corn. Short plants allow close spacing and the ears will keep for up to 2 weeks on the stalk without losing their flavor.
* **Silver Queen** — This white hybrid is the best corn I've ever eaten. It gives high yields of large, tender ears. It is, however, quite late. **Golden Queen Hybrid** is the same except for its color.
* **Seneca Chief** — An exceptionally tasty and tender yellow variety, slightly earlier than Golden Queen.
* **Kandy Corn and Mainliner** — Two of the new "EH", or Everlasting Heritage, varieties. The suffix "EH" means the conversion of sugar to starch is slowed down in the kernels which allows the picking

Golden Miniature is very early, producing an abundance of cobs on dwarf plants.

STOKES SEEDS LTD.

period to be extended by as much as 2 weeks.

- **Illinis Xtra-Sweet** — Excellent for freezing, this variety is twice as sweet as ordinary hybrids at picking time. The sweetness is retained for about 48 hours after harvest which takes place very late — mid-August in most areas.
- **Early Xtra-Sweet** — More uniform in appearance and 2 weeks earlier than Xtra-Sweet, this All-America winner is superior in sweetness and flavor.
- **Peaches and Cream** — Similar to **Honey and Cream** or **Butter and Sugar**, the ears feature bright kernels of both white and yellow together. Unique and attractive in appearance, it's also very tasty and yields heavily.
- **Popcorn** — A must for families with children. Popcorn takes considerably longer to mature than regular corn with the ideal time for planting in most areas being the last 2 weeks in May.
- **Strawberry Ornamental Popcorn** — In addition to popping, this variety makes an unusual addition to floral arrangements. The ears are an attractive mahogany red color.
- **Indian Ornamental Corn** — Grown strictly for decoration, each ear carries a remarkable range of colors. It will take 110 days to mature.
- **White Cloud Hulless** — Early, with strong hybrid vigor. The quality and popping performance of this variety is outstanding.

Cucumbers

Men have been growing cucumbers for centuries; they're mentioned in the Bible and in the earliest Chinese agricultural records. There are now more than 30 varieties available to the home gardener, and in the last 40 years North Americans have doubled their consumption. One of the major reasons for this renewed popularity is that cucumbers are low in calories (only 25 in a large cucumber) and high in nutrition. Cucumbers contain many vitamins, plus calcium, potassium, and a touch of magnesium. Another reason is that, in the last 20 years, cucumbers have undergone tremendous changes which have made them much easier to grow.

When I was a boy, all we had were the open-pollinated varieties which were subject to more diseases than almost any other vegetable. Modern hybrids have overcome this problem and now have a built-in resistance to the major cucumber diseases. Many new hybrids also produce only female flowers which means you'll get a much higher yield and the fruits will have fewer seeds than other varieties.

Preparation, Planting and Care

The soil in which you plan to set out your cucumbers should be rich, containing plenty of humus and a complete garden fertilizer, such as a 5-10-5 or a 4-12-8. You can't go wrong if you make sure each planting site is one-third to one-half humus. The easiest and best humus to use is one of the commercial brands of composted cattle manure.

SALADIN HYBRID CUCUMBERS — MEDIUM SIZED PICKLING FRUITS WITH NON-BITTER SKINS

The humus will open up and lighten heavier clays or act like a sponge in lighter sandy soils to retain moisture. Fertilizer should be applied to the surface of the soil and the humus spread on top of it. Thoroughly mix the humus, fertilizer and earth together down to a depth of 8in (20cm), using a garden spade or rotary tiller. Rake to level, removing any debris, and you're ready to plant.

A good plan is to start some cucumbers indoors 4 weeks before they can be set out in the garden in your area. Sow the seeds in peat-fibre, plastic or clay pots under fluorescent lights or in the sunniest window of your home. Started plants are also available from nurseries and garden centers but by growing your own you can always obtain the varieties you prefer.

Outdoors, the regular varieties of cucumber seed are sown in hills 4ft (1.2m) apart, allowing 5 seeds per hill. When the plants are 6in (15cm) high, thin them to 3 plants per hill. Seeds will germinate in 7 to 10 days, when the soil temperature reaches 65°F (18°C). You can also sow seeds 5in (12.5cm) apart in rows spaced 4ft (1.2m) apart, thinning the resulting plants so that they stand 12in (20cm) apart in the row.

Space can be saved in the smaller garden by growing the cucumbers up a fence or by using one of the plastic or string trellis nettings to train them up off the ground.

A second sowing at the beginning of July will assure a supply of cucumbers until the arrival of the first frosts of autumn. All cucumbers are ready for harvesting 2 months after the seeds go into the ground.

The cucumber plants are shallow-rooted and require plenty of moisture. Starting in early June, soak them well once a week. Leave the sprinkler in one place long enough to allow the water to penetrate to a depth of 5 to 6in (12.5 to 15cm).

Once the plants have really started to grow, give each one a feeding with a complete garden fertilizer (a 5-1-5 or a 4-8-12), applying half a cupful around each plant and working it gently into the surface of the earth with a Dutch hoe or a rake.

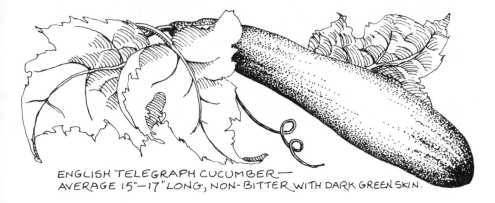
ENGLISH TELEGRAPH CUCUMBER—
AVERAGE 15"–17" LONG, NON-BITTER WITH DARK GREEN SKIN.

Bush cucumbers produce fruits freely on dwarf, mounded plants.

STOKES SEEDS LTD.

Gourmet Cucumbers

To accommodate the smaller garden, breeders have developed a new race of bush cucumbers which use only one-third the space of normal varieties yet yield a large and tasty crop. Follow the usual procedure for growing regular cucumbers, and use a soil mixture of 2 parts top soil to 1 part humus and 1 part builder's or gardener's sand. To each bushel (35L) of this mixture add a large handful of complete garden fertilizer, such as a 4-12-8 or 5-10-5. Bush cucumbers mature in 55 days.

- **Bush Champion** and **Bush Whopper** — Both varieties produce fruits freely on their dwarf, mounded plants. There are no runners and the vines are short. With Bush Whopper, unbelievably large cucumbers are produced for the size of the bush.

Of the regular varieties, I find the following to be first-class:
- **Patio Pik Hybrid** — A multi-purpose cucumber which can be used for pickling when young or for eating fresh when mature. The plants are compact and do well in small gardens or containers.
- **Sweet Slice Hybrid** — In the large cucumber class, these fruits are sweet, with no bitterness, and they're "burpless". The plants yield vigorously over a long season.
- **Saladin Hybrid** — An AAS winner, this all-female hybrid is resistant to cucumber mosaic and tolerant to powdery mildew and bacterial wilt. It's ideal for all types of pickles and delicious raw.
- **English Telegraph** — The best of the frame cucumbers for flavor, this is the cucumber to choose for growing on top of your home garden compost factory.

Eggplant

With each passing year, more and more people are becoming aware of eggplant as an interesting main ingredient in many gourmet dishes. For this reason, it's also becoming a very popular addition to the home garden. Eggplant comes to us originally from Asia and Africa.

The earliest eggplant [right] is the high-yielding Dusky.

Decorative, tasty little fruits are carried on Easter Egg [below].

STOKES SEEDS LTD.

BALL SUPERIOR, LTD.

Preparation, Planting and Care

Eggplants require exactly the same culture as tomatoes. The plants should be started indoors 8 to 10 weeks before the night temperatures are expected to be consistently above 55°F (13°C). (This is usually the last week in May or the first week in June.) For the seeds to germinate, the indoor temperature should be 70°F (21°C) and the process will take anywhere from 10 to 15 days.

Choose a sunny spot in your garden, making the soil rich and friable. Set the plants 2ft (60cm) apart in the row and keep 2ft (60cm) between the rows. Work a complete garden fertilizer, such as a 4-12-8 or a 5-10-5, into the earth before planting and feed once a month thereafter until the fruits are ready for eating. Give each plant a cup of special starter solution to get the plants off to a quick start and to lessen transplanting shock.

Gourmet Eggplant

- **Dusky** — A new hybrid variety which will provide a high yield over a long season. This is the eggplant to grow in regions where the frost-free season is short as it matures at least 10 days earlier than standard eggplants.
- **Black Beauty** — A common, large-fruited eggplant whose fruits are tender and tasty at all stages of maturity.
- **Pick-Me-Quick** — A small plant which produces a surprisingly large crop if continually picked. This is the ideal eggplant for growing in limited space or in containers.
- **Easter Egg** — This novelty plant looks as if it were bearing white hen's eggs which are really decorative and tasty little eggplants.

Jerusalem Artichokes

I wonder how many people have ever grown or even tasted the Jerusalem artichoke. Just to confuse things, it's not an artichoke at all, nor does it originate in Jerusalem. This tasty vegetable is cultivated for its tubers which are not unlike potatoes when steamed and served with butter, salt and pepper. The tubers can also be used for salads, relishes and pickles.

When boiled, the skins should be left on until you're ready to serve them. Cooking time will vary with the size, larger tubers taking about 30 minutes. The honey-flavored liquid which remains after boiling makes a pleasant drink when salt and herbs are added and it also provides diabetics with a harmless sugar substitute. If you're a diabetic, it's best to check with your doctor first.

The Jerusalem artichoke is one of the easiest of all vegetables to grow. It's tough and will do well in any kind of soil with good drainage. Naturally, the richer the soil, the better your results.

Tubers are available from most mail order seedhouses and from some garden centers and nurseries. For planting, use the largest tubers you can find. They should be treated like potatoes and cut into pieces with 3 or 4 eyes. Set the pieces 6in (15cm) deep, just as soon as the soil is workable in the spring. Space them 3ft (90cm) apart.

The tall foliage should be pinched back to prevent the flowers from forming in the summer. The tubers can be left in the ground until required. In early October, dig up those that remain, and store them in damp sand in the coolest part of the cellar. It won't hurt them a bit if the temperature is between 32 and 40°F (0-4°C).

Kohlrabi

Kohlrabi, an ancient and respected member of the cabbage family, was being grown in Roman gardens at the time of Pompeii. It's still a popular vegetable in all the countries of northern Europe, where it's grown for the attractive, swollen stems that resemble above-ground turnips.

Though it's still relatively uncommon, kohlrabi is coming into its own in the North American garden. First of all, it is particularly well-suited to our intensive style of gardening, producing lots of edible matter in very little space. Secondly, widespread interest was aroused when, in 1979, the **Grand Duke Hybrid** variety was honored with an All-America silver medal. Since then, many home gardeners have been adding a bit of European flavor to their gardens by planting kohlrabi.

The so-called "bulbs" of Grand Duke Hybrid can be peeled and sliced thin for dips, grated for salads, or diced for cooking. Their taste is mild, sweet and crunchy, with no hint of toughness. When the small inner leaves are cooked together with the roots they have a delectable taste similar to kale or any of the collard greens and are laden with vitamins. In preparation for cooking, the side leaves should be pulled off and the roots peeled from the bottom up. Sliced or diced, kohlrabi may be blanched and frozen with no difficulty.

Grand Duke was bred for quick maturing, so there is little to be gained from starting plants indoors. Seeds can be set out in the garden while it's still cold, as long as the soil is workable. They'll sprout in about 5 to 7 days and be ready for eating 45 to 50 days after seeding. The hybrid vigor of Grand Duke will carry it through spells of adverse weather which would hinder the growth of ordinary varieties. Under almost any conditions, this breed will reward you with fat, round stems, 3 to 4in (7.5 to 10cm) in diameter.

Preparation, Planting and Care

A rich soil, containing plenty of humus and fertilizer, will assure the formation of a "bulb" on virtually every plant. Add the same kind and amount of humus and fertilizer to the soil as previously recommended for carrots and beets.

It's possible to get 2 crops of kohlrabi if you sow as soon as the earth is workable and again late in July. You'll then be able to harvest

STOKES SEEDS LTD.

Bred for quick maturing, Grand Duke thrives under almost any conditions.

by the end of June and again around the middle of September. The late summer planting means that the plants will be maturing in cool weather which will intensify their sweetness. They will tolerate a light frost but when hard frost threatens the plants should be covered with leaves held down by a piece of plastic. Kohlrabi is a valuable substitute root crop in gardens where insects would bore into white turnips and rutabagas. Bulbs grown in the fall can also be pulled and stored under a deep layer of straw in a coldframe.

Lettuce

In these calorie-conscious days, people are eating far more salads and taking a renewed interest in growing their own lettuce. The Greeks gave lettuce to the Romans, who introduced it to Britain and from there it travelled to North America.

You'll not only save considerable money by growing your own lettuce, but you'll be able to produce the delicious loosehead or looseleaf varieties.

Preparation, Planting and Care

All types of lettuce have a relatively poor root system. For this reason, it's imperative that the earth next to the roots contain plenty of humus and fertilizer. Before you plant, make the earth one-third humus and add a generous amount of complete garden fertilizer such as a 4-12-8 or a 5-10-5, at the rate recommended by the manufacturer. Work the soil, humus and fertilizer together thoroughly down to a depth of 6in (15cm). Rake level to remove any debris, and you're ready to plant.

In early March a few plants can be started in peat-fibre, clay or plastic pots to be set out in the garden or placed in a large container on the balcony or patio. Whether the seeds are sown indoors or outdoors, don't cover them with earth as you would with most flowers and vegetables. Lettuce seed needs light to germinate and will take anywhere from 7 to 10 days to produce seedlings.

Indoor gardeners can have a supply of looseleaf lettuce coming along all year. Fill a 6in (15cm) container with potting soil, levelling it so that the surface of the soil is 1/2in (1cm) below the rim of the container. Scatter the seeds thickly over the surface, but don't cover them. Soak thoroughly with room-temperature water and place the container in a well-lit location or under a fluorescent light set-up. As soon as the plants are 4in (10cm) high, you can start using them; just cut off the leaves with a pair of scissors.

There's little doubt that the best way to grow the loosehead and looseleaf varieties is to sow the seed in the open, just as soon as the earth is workable, and follow up with a succession of plantings every 2 weeks until the beginning of August.

Sow the seeds in drills 1/4in (.5cm) deep and 12in (30cm) apart and do not cover as they need light to germinate. Once the new seedlings are 1in (2.5cm) high you can fill in the furrows to give the seedlings more support. Again, just as soon as the lettuce plants are 3 to 4in (7.5 to 10cm) high, you can start thinning them and use the delicious leaves for salads or sandwiches. The remaining plants should be 8in (20cm) apart in the row.

The soil in which lettuce is planted should be moist at all times, which means you must give it a good soaking once a week without fail. Leave the sprinkler in place long enough for the water to penetrate to a depth of 6in (15cm) and every 3 weeks use a soluable, complete garden fertilizer.

You'll probably have trouble getting lettuce seed to germinate outside in mid-summer, particularly if the temperature is above 80°F (27°C). Instead, mix the lettuce seed with damp sand or peat moss and store it in the vegetable bin of your refrigerator for a week. After you take the mixture out, the seeds should be sown immediately in the normal way, leaving them uncovered. Seedlings will then be readily produced and will grow strongly.

Gourmet Loosehead Lettuce

The plants of the loosehead varieties form a round, thick bunch of leaves which are blanched to a light green or creamy yellow in the center of the head. The leaves are attractive, tender, mild and delightfully crisp. You can start thinning the plants and using the leaves when they are just a few inches (8 to 10cm) high.

- **Buttercrunch** — Correctly called the "ideal" home garden lettuce, this All-America winner is vigorous, dependable and easy to grow. The eating quality, particularly of the heart, is superb.
- **Butter King** — One of the largest loosehead lettuces, the heads are extremely uniform and highly resistant to disease, tip-burn and blight.
- **Tom Thumb** — A midget sized butterhead variety, perfect for containers, window boxes or hobby greenhouses. The compact heads can be served whole or cut in half for individual salads.

Gourmet Looseleaf Lettuce

The looseleaf varieties probably give the fastest, most generous return for the least amount of money, care and garden space. They will grow indoors under fluorescent lighting or in the hobby greenhouse and be ready for eating just 4 or 5 weeks from sowing.

- **Salad Bowl** — Undoubtedly the best looseleaf lettuce for the home garden is this AAS gold medal winner. It holds its fine flavor and texture despite summer heat and 3 sowings will provide enough lettuce over the gardening season for the average family.

The color and sweetness of its leaves make Ruby Red [above] well-worth growing.

Butter King [right] is one of the largest and hardiest looseleaf lettuces.

- **Red Salad Bowl** — Similar to the regular Salad Bowl except that it displays a rich reddish tone wherever it has been touched by the sun.
- **Ruby Red** — Another AAS winner, well-worth growing for its unusual red color and sweet, succulant leaves. It won't fade in hot weather and is resistant to tip-burn.

Unusual Salad Vegetables

While lettuce is undoubtedly the most common main ingredient in salads, there are a number of rather exotic vegetables which offer something a little different to the gourmet home gardener.

Celtuce

Burpee's Celtuce, although not too widely grown, is a versatile vegetable whose flavor is a delectable combination of celery and lettuce. It's a member of the lettuce family, producing leaves for use in salads or as tasty greens. Celtuce has 4 times the vitamin C content of head lettuce. The elongated center stalk reaches about 15in (40cm) in length and 1-1/2in (4cm) in diameter. It's tender and succulent whether eaten raw or cooked like asparagus.

Celtuce is easy to grow, withstands more heat than head lettuce and

The flavor of Burpee's Celtuce [above] is a delicate combination of celery and lettuce.

Witloof chicory [right] makes a delicious and interesting salad vegetable.

W. ATLEE BURPEE CO.

ROYAL SLUIS

LAMB'S LETTUCE/FETTICUS – ALSO KNOWN AS CORN SALAD.

doesn't seriously tip-burn in the summer heat. You can sow it in the garden as you would lettuce and small, successive sowings made 4 weeks apart will provide a supply of leaves and hearts right up to the first hard frost of autumn.

Lamb's Lettuce/Fetticus

Lamb's lettuce, or fetticus, is a fine, long-season salad plant that grows quickly and easily from seed. Within 60 days from sowing you'll be able to use the first delicious leaves. They have a very delicate taste, perfect for salads. When cooked like spinach or Swiss chard, lamb's lettuce makes excellent greens.

Preparation for planting is the same as for carrots and beets. A first sowing can be made just as soon as the earth is workable in the spring, followed by repeated sowings 3 weeks apart until the middle of August. In containers in the hobby greenhouse or under special lighting, lamb's lettuce is a simple crop to grow. The first leaves will be ready for use when they're 5 to 6in (12.5 to 15cm) high.

Witloof Chicory/Belgian Endive

Every year great quantities of Belgian endive, or Witloof chicory, are imported for gourmet cooks who value it as a delicious and interesting salad vegetable. It's easy to grow in your own garden, though, and at a fraction of the cost.

Seed is sown outdoors in May or early June and from then until October they'll develop roots to produce the large, tender stalks or sprouts which appear once the plants are taken indoors and forced. They should be dug out, the tops trimmed and the roots stored in moist sand in a warm, dark place. The mail order seedhouses usually send complete directions for raising this crop with each order of seeds.

Onions

Onions are universally well-liked as a flavorful addition to salads, soups and stews, or as a main vegetable both cooked and raw. They also store extremely well and can provide year-round eating enjoyment.

Onions, shallots, chives, leeks, and many of their relatives originated in central Asia and are members of the widespread Lily family. The Egyptians placed great value on onions; the Children of Israel cried out for them during their journey across the desert; and in the Middle Ages, onions were thought to be a heaven-sent cure for everything from deafness to baldness because their shape resembled that of the human head. After their introduction to North America by early Spanish explorers, onions soon became a very important vegetable in the settlers' diet.

Preparation, Planting and Care
Onion Sets

To get the earliest possible green onions or mature bulbs with the least amount of trouble, use top-quality onion sets. These are really small bulbs, especially grown for the purpose of yielding an early crop. They're generally available in Vexar, or other types of bags, from all the usual sources.

For the many people who now garden on a balcony or patio, onion sets offer an opportunity to grow a steady supply of green onions from late May until the hard frosts of autumn. Fill a large container, such as half a wooden barrel, with one of the commercial potting soils. Plant half of it with onion sets early in April, spacing then 1in (2.5cm) apart. Three weeks later, plant the other half. From then on, replant each time the onions in one half of the container have been consumed.

Planted indoors, onion sets should be given plenty of sun or grown under fluorescent lights. The bulbs themselves will contain all the food required to develop edible green onions. By using 2 medium-sized containers a constant supply can be obtained year-round.

Onions always need planting in a well-drained, fertile soil which contains plenty of humus and a complete garden fertilizer, such as a 4-12-8 or 5-10-5. Use the same amounts of humus and fertilizer and prepare the soil in the same way as you would for beans and carrots.

As soon as the earth is workable in the spring, make a furrow 1in (2.5cm) deep and lightly press the sets into the bottom and cover them with earth. Space them 1in (2.5cm) apart for green onions, and 3in (7.5cm) apart if you intend to harvest large, mature bulbs. I like to space them 1in (2.5cm) apart at planting time and use every other plant as a green onion. Those that remain, I leave to mature. By the last 2 weeks in July, the onions should be a good size for cooking and when the tops go down in August they can be harvested for eating fresh or for winter storage.

Main Crop Onions

Main crop onions can easily be grown from seed in the garden. Just as soon as the ground can be worked in the spring, sow the seed in furrows 1/2in (1cm) deep. Germination should take place in 10 days. When the resulting plants are 3in (7.5cm) high, thin them to 3in (7.5cm) apart. Seedlings grown indoors under fluorescent lights in early March will be ready for transplanting by May, or you can purchase started plants at this time. As the bulbs mature in late summer, bend the tops down to hasten their ripening. After removing the mature bulbs from the ground, lay them on the surface of the earth, allowing them to dry for several days. Sun-cured onions will always store much better.

Every year, thousands of tons of onions go to waste through spoilage. In storing onions, cold temperatures will cause rot while high temperatures will cause them to sprout. Since the refrigerator is too cold, the best solution is to keep your onions in the cellar or in some other suitable storage area.

Scallions/Green Onions

There are some types of perennial scallions, or green onions, which do not form bulbs, remain in the ground for years, and can be used at any stage in their growth. Seeds sown in spring or summer will produce long, white tender scallions for fall use. If kept over the winter, they will provide the finest green onions even earlier than onion sets. Although they're hardy, it's a good idea to cover these perennials during the winter with a 3in (7.5cm) mulch of humus.

Gourmet Onions

- **Sweet Spanish** — All major seed houses will carry this variety or one of its hybrids. The onions are mild, sweet and fine-grained but store only moderately well.
- **Patti King** — A hybrid of the Sweet Spanish, this variety can be harvested earlier and will keep well into the winter. The name refers to its use as the ideal hamburger garnish.

Sweet spanish onions are mild and fine-grained.

- **Yellow Globe Hybrid** — Outstanding in its earliness, uniformity and high yield, its exceptional keeping quality makes this variety the best for winter storage.
- **Spartan Sleeper** — A remarkable long-life storage onion that will remain firm and crisp from late summer until the following spring at normal room temperature. They can be bunched together and hung in the kitchen for a decorative effect with no risk of spoilage.
- **White Portugal** — The best type of silverskin onion to grow for pickling. To keep the succulent bulbs small, sow the seed 1/2 in (1 cm) deep and very thick.
- **Red Sunset** — This Fl hybrid is one of the best red onions. Much like a Sweet Spanish, it is vigorous, uniform and of outstanding quality.

Parsnips

This nutritious root vegetable with its nutty flavor has been grown since Roman times and I'm happy to report that parsnips are regaining their popularity with home gardeners. I find they make a welcome alternative to beans, beets, potatoes and carrots. The parsnip is a biennial vegetable that can be left in the ground over the winter. In fact, their flavor is considerably improved by frost.

To grow parsnips, the earth must be very well prepared. Add the same amount of humus and fertilizer to the soil as you would for beans or carrots, thoroughly mixing them together with the earth down to a depth of 10in (25cm). Rake 2 or 3 times to level the ground and completely pulverize the soil, getting rid of any debris.

The seeds should never be sown in over 1/4in (.5cm) of soil and then barely covered. Thin the resulting plants to 4in (10cm) apart when they reach 2in (5cm) in height. I usually sow a block of 6sq ft (.5sq m) and cover it with a 3in (7.5cm) layer of humus in October. I then place a cold-frame over the bed. In so doing, you can use the highly edible roots well into the winter and, after the first freeze, dig out the others for storage in a deep outdoor pit or in moist sand in the root cellar. Still more parsnips can be left in the ground over the winter and eaten as soon as the frost is out of the ground in the spring.

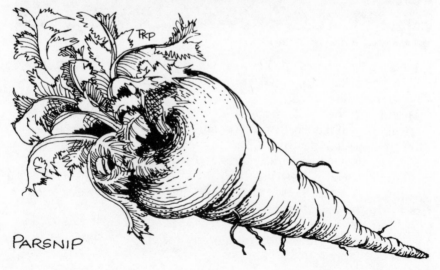

PARSNIP

Peanuts

Anyone with children will find it amusing to grow a few hills of peanuts. They will grow surprisingly well in the home garden, provided the soil is on the light side — you won't get good results from a heavy clay. The best peanut for home gardeners to grow is the early maturing Spanish variety.

Planting time is in May, when the soil has warmed up. The peanuts will require the same germination and growing temperatures as sweet corn so they'll need a frost-free growing season of 4 months.

Unroasted nuts should be purchased from a seed house, shelled and sown 2in (5cm) deep and 6in (15cm) apart. When the young plants are 2 to 3in (5 to 7.5cm) high, thin them to 12in (30cm) apart. Where peanuts are to be grown in quantity, 30in (75cm) should be left between each row.

Peanuts should be hilled up with earth once the nuts begin to form. Just before autumn frost, dig up the entire plant with the peanuts still attached to the roots and hang them in a warm, airy place to cure. Anyone with a large container on a balcony or patio could grow 3 to 4 clumps and enjoy the fun of showing them to children and friends.

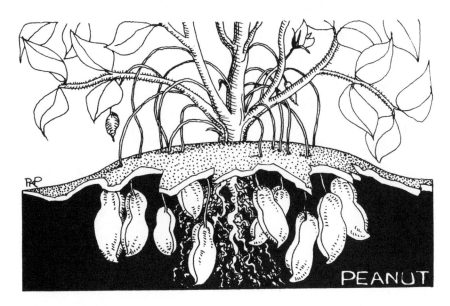

PEANUT

STOKES SEEDS LTD.

The pods and peas of Sugar Snap [above] both make for delicious eating.
The double-podded Green Arrow [below] provides high yields in limited space.

STOKES SEEDS LTD.

Peas

To my way of thinking there's no other vegetable quite so delicious as tender, young peas. Especially when they've gone straight from the garden, small and full of sugar, into the cooking pot. Fast-frozen commercial peas may have an advantage over the canned ones, but there's still no substitute for your own garden-fresh pods or those you freeze yourself.

The pea family has over 12,000 members and is the world's second most important group of edible plants. It's no wonder, then, that mankind has been savoring them for such a very long time. In the cooler parts of Europe and Western Asia where they originated, they go back thousands of years. In fact, the garden pea was a popular family vegetable in the Stone Age.

Preparation, Planting and Care

Beginners to gardening should know that both the garden pea and the sweet pea relish cool weather and need to be planted just as soon as the soil is workable in the spring. The latest research shows that peas can go into the ground once the soil temperature reaches 39°F (4°C). I sow peas as early as possible because hot weather, at the time when peas are developing in the pods, will cause a severe reduction in yield. Although pea seeds will germinate at 39°F (4°C) or higher, the optimum temperature for germination and early growth is 68°F (20°C).

Early germination is frequently exasperatingly slow. Often, the newcomer to gardening is just giving up hope that his seeds will ever germinate when he discovers that Nature has once again worked one of her miracles. On the first warm spring morning, the burgeoning new seedlings will have pushed their way through the earth and at least 95 per cent of them will have germinated.

You can easily get a jump on the season by germinating the seeds needed for the first sowing in a roll of wet flannel. Another excellent method is to sow the seeds in peat fibre, clay or plastic pots 3 weeks ahead of the time you expect the soil to become workable, moving the plants to the garden when they're 2 to 3in (5 to 7.5cm) high.

The roots of peas and other legumes are covered with tiny nodules which host a special strain of bacteria. This bacteria takes the nitrogen gas from the air and changes it into a form the plants can use for food.

You can help develop this nitrogen-fixing ability by treating the seed with innoculants just before planting. To the beginner, treating the seed may seem like a complicated process, but it can easily be done in two ways. These legume aids are widely available in the form of a black powder. You can either soak the seeds in water briefly and then dip them in the powder, or you can dust it along the furrow just before planting. I prefer the latter method.

Peas are vigorous growers and will require an ample and uniform supply of moisture. Your job is to make sure that the earth in which they're planted contains plenty of humus and fertilizer to meet this important need.

Peas need a complete garden fertilizer, such as a 4-12-8 or 5-10-5, worked into the earth just before seeding. This will supply a balanced amount of nitrogen, phosphorus, and potash in the soil. Nitrogen promotes the green growth, phosphorous the root growth, and potash the overall health of the plants. Scatter the fertilizer over the soil at a rate of 4lbs (1.8kg) per 100sq ft (9sq m) or follow the specific directions of the manufacturer.

Next, with your garden spade or rotary tiller, mix the earth, humus and fertilizer down to a depth of 8in (20cm). Give the earth a final levelling with the garden rake and remove any debris before you sow.

In most gardens, pea seeds are sown in a furrow 3in (7.5cm) deep, but in very light soils the planting depth should be increased to 4in (10cm). Three sowings, 2 weeks apart, will help to ensure that all the peas won't mature at once. The picking season can also be lengthened somewhat by selecting several varieties of peas, each maturing at a different time.

Just as soon as the plants are 2 to 3in (5 to 7.5cm) high, give them a second fertilizer feeding. Cultivate shallowly with a Dutch hoe, to work the fertilizer into the earth and to eliminate any weeds, then soak the earth to a depth of 5 to 6in (12.5 to 15cm). A mulch of humus 3in (7.5cm) deep should be applied next along both sides of the row. Grass clippings, composted cattle manure, clean wheat straw, material from the home garden compost factory, peat moss or discarded mushroom manure make excellent mulches for peas. The mulch will keep the roots cool, eliminate weeds, and preserve the soil's moisture.

From late May onwards, give the peas a good soaking with the hose once a week, so the water penetrates to a depth of 5 to 6in (12.5 to 15cm).

Gourmet Garden Peas
- **Little Marvel** — Its earliness, exceptional quality and high yield have made this the most outstanding early pea for over 100 years. Vines grow high and need no support.

- **Lincoln/Homesteader** — A hardy, disease-resistant variety to use for later sowings as it will withstand summer heat to produce high yields. Vigorous vines will need staking.
- **Sugar Snap** — A truly outstanding new pea and winner of the AAS gold medal. Delicious pods and peas can both be eaten, providing twice the edible matter per row as normal shell peas. The pods will remain in prime eating condition for days, unlike the Snow Pea which it has effectively replaced. Vines will be tall and need support.
- **Sugar Bon** — A bush version of Sugar Snap which does not need staking.
- **Novella** — An entirely new dwarf-vined pea which can support itself if planted in a double row. Two pods are produced at the site of most blossom nodes, creating a very high yield.
- **Green Arrow** — Another double-podded type which makes for easy picking of heavy crops in limited space. Unusually long pods of select quality can be successfully frozen.
- **Petit Pois** — The true small-seeded French pea can withstand hard frosts and earth that has frozen up to 2in (5cm) deep. Vines require staking or trellising.

Asparagus Peas

Another uncommon gourmet vegetable I like is the asparagus pea. It's not a true pea, but is related to the Lotus and is handsome enough to use as an annual ground cover. The brownish-red pods resemble those of the regular garden pea and grow in a curious winged manner at maturity. The pods are gathered and cooked whole when they're 1-1/2 to 2 in (3.5 to 5cm) in length and their flavor is a cross between garden peas and asparagus.

You'll find that the asparagus pea is quite sensitive to cold soil and air temperaturers. Don't put the seeds into the ground until the last week of May or the first week in June and they'll need to be located in full sun. Sow the seeds so that the resulting plants will be 15in (40cm) apart. The bushes will reach 1-1/2ft (45cm) at maturity.

Ornamental Sweet Banana peppers are ideal for salads and frying

Peppers

The tropical areas of the Americas have given us the versatile pepper. Many people are not aware that most varieties of peppers, both hot and sweet, will turn red at maturity. Sweet peppers, however, are usually picked green, as soon as they're firm and have reached a good size.

Thick-walled California Wonder is the most popular garden pepper.

Preparation, Planting and Care

For peppers, choose a location that receives full sun and use a soil that's rich in humus and fertilizer. Two feedings will be required using a complete garden fertilizer such as a 4-12-8 or a 5-10-5. The first should be worked into the earth with the humus before planting and the second should be given 6 weeks later. Soak thoroughly once a week and put a 3in (7.5cm) mulch in place toward the last week in June.

Gourmet Sweet Peppers

- **California Wonder** — The most popular garden pepper and one of the best varieties to use for stuffed peppers because of its thick walls.
- **Gypsy Hybrid** — An incredibly productive All-America winner, it is a rare combination of earliness, fruit quality and heavy production. The compact plants are extremely decorative grown in the garden or in containers.
- **Dutch Treat** — Another AAS winner, this is an attractively formed, colorful pepper of outstanding quality which will grow almost anywhere.
- **Sweet Banana** — Bright red when fully mature, these long, tapered peppers are highly ornamental as well as being ideal for salads or frying.
- **Early Pimento** — This beautiful scarlet, heart-shaped pepper won an All-America award on its introduction. The heavy-walled fruits freeze very well.

Gourmet Hot Peppers

- **Long Red Cayenne** — These spicy, pungent fruits are often curled and twisted. No other variety is as hot and the fruits are easily dried for year-round use.
- **Hungarian Wax** — A very popular pepper, relatively early and moderately hot.
- **Zippy Hybrid** — The earliest of all peppers, the plants are sturdy and a colorful addition to a flower border. They dry well for winter use and are zesty but not fiery hot.

Potatoes

There's nothing more delectable than a new potato, right from the garden, that's been boiled with a few sprigs of fresh mint. It's not surprising, then, that the potato is one of our most popular vegetables.

The potatoes we grow in our gardens originated in the mountains of Central America where they were cultivated as early as 200 A.D. Spanish explorers took them to Europe in the late 1600's and in the next century they were among those plants brought to North America by early settlers.

A number of hills of new potatoes are a must for the bigger garden, but it really doesn't pay to grow large amounts for winter storage when they will be readily available in the supermarket at comparatively low prices. Two plantings made a month apart will provide the home gardener with all the new potatoes he'll need from early July until sometime in September.

Preparation, Planting and Care

Potatoes are a cool weather crop that will tolerate a light frost, so it's safe to plant as soon as the earth becomes workable and 2 weeks before the last killing frost can be expected in your area. Don't plant in earth that is less than 45°F (7°C), though, as this will delay the start of growth and can cause rotting.

Tubers will begin to form 40 to 50 days after planting and, at about the same time, the plants will start to flower. This blooming has nothing to do with the development of the tubers, however. The vigor and health of the top growth is the determining factor in how early the tubers are formed and how large the crop will be.

It may surprise you to know that the potato belongs to the same botanical family as tomatoes, peppers and eggplants. You should therefore prepare the soil for planting potatoes as you would for these other vegetables, working in plenty of humus and a complete garden fertilizer.

The home gardener how has a choice of 3 ways to grow potatoes. You can plant in the traditional way using chunky pieces of potato weighing about 1-1/2oz (42gm) and each containing several eyes; you can use potato eyes carried by the better mail order seed companies or nurseries and garden outlets; or you can grow them from seed and treat them the same way as tomato or cabbage transplants.

The best advice I can give the home gardener purchasing seed potatoes or eyes is to imitate the commercial growers and use stock which has been certified by the government. Such stock is grown specifically for use by commercial growers and home gardeners. It must meet rigid standards and be disease-free. Never use table potatoes from the supermarket. These may grow and yield satisfactorily but they can be infected with diseases which don't exhibit any visible signs on the tubers. Such diseases will have no effect on the eating quality of the potatoes, but will most certainly mean a smaller and poorer crop.

Set the tubers 4in (10cm) deep and space them 12in (30cm) apart. Make the rows 30in (75cm) from each other. In 2 to 3 weeks, the new plants will emerge from the soil.

A good soaking once a week from the beginning of June onwards is vital to potatoes; lack of adequate moisture is the main cause of reduced yields. The sprinkler should be left in one place long enough for the water to penetrate the earth to a depth of 6in (15cm).

Weeds will compete fiercely with the potato plants for food, water and light. They're also potential hosts for disease and insect pests that attack potatoes. It's vital, then, to start hoeing as soon as the first weeds begin to sprout from the earth. One good hoeing before they have fully emerged is worth several later on. Continue hoeing once a week until the potato plants start to bloom. Hilling the earth up around the plants will smother any weeds next to them and prevent greening of the tubers by exposure to the sun. Begin hilling when the plants are 6in (15cm) high, making sure that you don't injure the roots or the developing tubers. Make the hills broad and flat, about 3 to 4in (7.5 to 10cm) high.

A month after the plants appear, when they're about 6in (15cm) high, give them a second feeding. Scatter the fertilizer along both sides of the row 2 to 3in (5 to 7.5cm) from the plants. Work it gently into the soil using a Dutch hoe or a garden rake.

Growing From Seed, Explorer
Until 1981, potatoes had to be grown from eyes or larger pieces of a potato tuber, as described above. This is no longer the case. Thanks to extensive research done in China, Peru and the United States, we now have Explorer, the first potato which can truly be grown from seed. It is available through the better mail order seed companies but, at the time of writing, Explorer is still in the experimental stages. I would recommend using the old methods until it has been thoroughly tested in the home garden.

Explorer is a light russet potato which will do well in any climate

The light russet Explorer is the first potato to be grown from seed.

where potatoes normally grow. The seeds are started indoors, in a sunny window, under a fluorescent light set-up or in a hobby greenhouse 6 weeks before the usual planting time for potatoes. The started plants are set out 3 to a hill, the hills being spaced 18in (45cm) apart and the rows kept 30in (75cm) from each other. Small new potatoes will be ready for eating 90 days after planting and you'll have mature potatoes 30 days later. Doubtless the development of Explorer is the start of a major new trend in growing potatoes, and we'll be hearing more about it in the near future.

Gourmet Potatoes

The varieties you choose will depend mainly on the climate in your area. Nurseries, garden outlets, government agricultural representatives and local garden clubs can provide information to help in your selection.

- **White or Irish Cobbler** — The most popular of all the white potatoes, it yields an early crop, has superior flavor and is excellent for baking.
- **Red Pontiac** — The leading variety of the newly popular red potatoes that does well even in heavy soils. It yields an early to mid-season crop of all-purpose, smooth-textured potatoes.
- **Kennebec** — The most popular all-purpose potato not only for its smooth texture and white flesh, but for its outstanding resistance to late blight. It is a mid-season, high-yield crop.

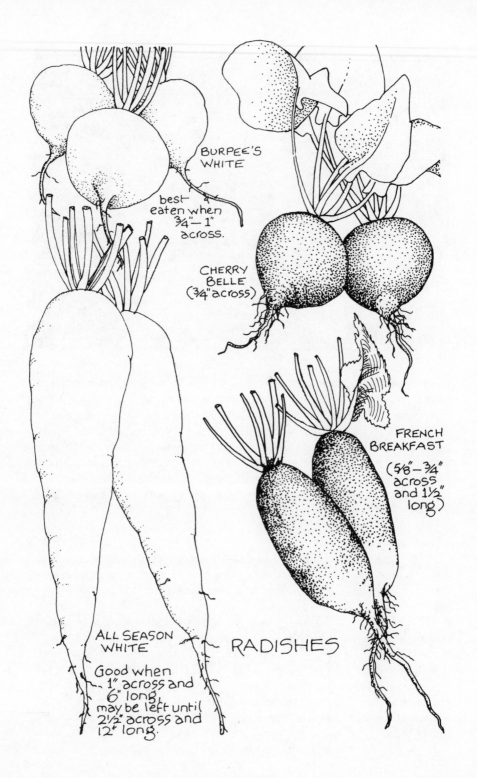

BURPEE'S
WHITE

best
eaten when
3/4" — 1"
across.

CHERRY
BELLE
(3/4" across)

FRENCH
BREAKFAST

(5/8" – 3/4"
across
and 1 1/2"
long)

ALL SEASON
WHITE

Good when
1" across and
6" long,
may be left until
2 1/2" across and
12" long.

RADISHES

Radishes

The Romans were indirectly responsible for our cultivation of this delectable and ornamental vegetable. During the 5 centuries that they occupied Britain, they brought many plants from their homeland — some of them quite exotic. It was the early settlers from England who brought the radish to North America.

Not only will radishes grow virtually anywhere, but when freshly picked are a most exciting stimulant to the taste buds. Another advantage to growing radishes is that you can leave on an inch (2.5cm) or so of the attractive green tops when serving them, improving both the appearance and the flavor.

Preparation, Planting and Care

The sweetest and most crisp radishes are always grown as quickly as possible in the early spring or fall. The soil should be a sandy loam containing plenty of humus. All varieties grown in the western hemisphere take from 3 weeks to a month from seeding to harvesting.

The first seeds should be put into the ground just as soon as the earth is workable in the spring. Your earliest crop can serve a dual purpose, marking the rows of slower growing vegetables such as beets, carrots, parsley or parsnips. Simply mix some of the radish seeds together with the others.

Starting 2 weeks after the first sowing, begin to plant a 10ft (3m) row every 2 weeks until the 1st of June. Then repeat the process beginning in the middle of August, continuing until around the 20th of September. You'll have a plentiful supply of radishes all season.

Sow the seeds 1/2in (1cm) deep in finely prepared earth and thin the young seedlings to 2in (5cm) apart once they reach a height of 2in (5cm). Unless rainfall is heavy, a good soaking with the hose every week will improve the eating quality.

Root maggots which often attack radishes can be easily controlled by spraying a recommended insecticide along the furrow at planting time.

Gourmet Radishes

- **Burpee's White** — An unusual radish, well-known for its extreme tenderness, mildness and crispness. The roots stay in prime eating condition for quite a long time.

The attractive French Breakfast is a mild and tender radish.

- **Cherry Belle and Fancy Red** — Two red equivalents to Burpee's White. Cherry Belle is the earliest of all radishes and an All-America winner. Fancy Red has a unique multiple disease tolerance. Both are uniform in shape and of excellent quality.
- **French Breakfast** — A very attractive radish whose crisp, white flesh is mildly pungent and tender.
- **Summer Cross** — One of the large oriental radishes, this Japanese Fl hybrid was bred for heat tolerance and can be sowed in late spring or mid-summer. Eating quality and appearance of the roots are superb.
- **Japanese Nerima** — Another oriental variety which is probably the most delicious radish you'll ever taste. It grows to an immense size, often reaching a weight of 3lbs (1.4kg) or more.
- **All Season** — Really a brand new type of vegetable, it is delicious and distinctly different from either normal or oriental radishes. It may be used at all stages of growth, from spring through fall, and will store all winter in the refrigerator or cellar.

Salsify/Vegetable Oyster

One of the most unusual vegetables is salsify, or the vegetable oyster. Now that marine oysters are so expensive, white salsify can provide a delightful substitute for that delicate but distinctive flavor.

ROYAL SLUIS

Black salsify is a versatile and hardy vegetable.

Salsify is grown in exactly the same way as carrots or parsnips, with one sowing being made in the early spring and another being made in mid-June for a fall crop. The taste is always finer and more pronounced after the first frost of autumn. Salsify produced from the second sowing can remain in the ground over the winter without being harmed. In fact, such leftover roots will be even more tasty the following spring.

The first leaves produced from the spring sowing can be cut when they're about 6in (15cm) long, for use in salads or as greens. The best way to handle white salsify from the late seeding is to use some of the roots fresh, store some of them in moist sand in a cool cellar for winter eating, and leave the remainder for spring use. It's also quite possible, in early April, to place a coldframe or a season extender over some of those left in the garden and get a 3 week jump on the season.

Salsify roots are not peeled before cooking. They should be steamed for an hour, the skin scraped off and then cut into rounds for pan or deep-frying. They can be added to soups or boiled and eaten like carrots and parsnips. Try serving salsify with a cream or tartar sauce.

One Package of seed will sow a 15ft (4.5m) row and an ounce (28gm) will sow 100ft (30m). Seeds should be set 1/2in (1cm) deep and thinned to 3in (7.5cm) apart as soon as the young plants are 2in (5cm) high.

Black salsify is also well-worth growing. During the Middle Ages in Europe it was one of the most valued vegetables, thought to be a powerful tonic and medicine. It's one of the few vegetables that shouldn't be cultivated or disturbed in any way. Weeds which may appear should be removed at once by hand. When you disturb the roots they will become forked.

Seeds are put into the ground 1/2in (1cm) deep, just as soon as it can be worked in the spring. The roots will be mature by September or early October and at that time use some of them for eating fresh. Leave the rest in the ground, covered by a 2in (5cm) mulch, and they can be dug as needed well into late autumn. The remaining roots may stay in the earth throughout the winter for use in the early spring.

Squash

Cultivated squash dates back further in history than almost any other garden vegetable. Archaeologists have discovered stems, fruits, and seeds in cliff dwellings which would indicate that man was growing squash as long ago as 6,000 B.C. Today, it is the fifth most popular vegetable in North America and the demand for squash seed is increasing rapidly. This is due in part to the development of new varieties of winter squash whose compact vines fit into the small garden, and partly because summer squash has become a fashionable salad vegetable. In addition, squash is easy to grow almost anywhere, it's nutritious, low in calories, and can be eaten in so many different ways that entire cookbooks have been devoted to the subject.

The squash family tree is confusing to home gardeners and scientists alike. Squash is part of a much larger botanical family which includes cucumbers, watermelons, muskmelons, cantalopes, and pumpkins.

The most common way of classifying squash is to divide them into summer and winter types. Summer squash includes zucchini and vegetable marrow, both customarily eaten at an immature stage when the seeds are not fully developed and the rind is still tender. Winter squash is harvested and eaten when fully mature, after the rind has hardened. This makes them ideal for winter storage.

Preparation, Planting and Care

There's little doubt that squash is one of the easiest vegetables to grow if you keep in mind that they're like melons and are of tropical or sub-tropical origin. This means that they thrive when the days are hot and humid and nights are warm. Squash won't tolerate freezing or even cool temperatures and should therefore be planted only when the danger of frost is past, in late spring, and when the soil temperature is above 60°F (16°C).

Under ideal conditions, squash vines grow rapidly. Summer squash can produce edible fruits within 7 or 8 weeks from sowing. The winter, or baking, squash requires considerably more time, taking from 80 to 120 days to produce mature, hard-shelled fruits.

In all but the short season areas, 2 plantings of summer squash should be made. While squash planted in the spring may live through a

The unique Burpee Golden zucchini has a distinctively delicious flavor.

Unlike most scallop squashes, Peter Pan Hybrid may be eaten young or old.

long summer, it won't produce as high a yield as planting a second crop around the 20th of June. Winter squash planted in late spring will develop mature fruits just before the freezing weather arrives in the late fall in all but the short season areas.

Squash will grow in any well-drained and aerated soil but, because they are such heavy feeders, these vegetables need to be given a generous amount of complete garden fertilizer (a 4-12-8 or a 5-10-5) before sowing, and the soil should be one-third humus.

Started plants are available from some garden centers and nurseries, but they offer no advantage over squash seeds sown directly in the garden. Sizeable greenhouse plants are often not very hardy and suffer quite a setback when put outside. Seeds started indoors under fluorescent lights are a different matter. Once the seedlings are 2 to 3in (5 to 7.5cm) high, you can start putting them outside on warm days and bringing them back in at night. Seeds should be planted in 3 to 4in (7.5 to 10cm) pots 3 weeks before you plan to put them in the garden. It's a good idea to use peat pots because they can go directly into the ground thus minimizing root disturbance and transplanting shock.

In the garden, sow the seeds quite close together in hills. The young seedlings will then be able to help each other break through the earth. The hills should be low mounds of earth raised 6in (15cm) above the surface of the garden, to improve drainage and provide warmer soil. For compact varieties of squash, the hills should be spaced 30in (75cm) apart and the rows 3ft (90cm) apart. Varieties which produce runners or vines should be placed in hills 3ft (90cm) apart with 6ft (1.8m) left between rows.

Home gardeners are rediscovering a growing technique first used by the American Indians. Runner or vining types of squash and pumpkins

Jersey Golden Acorn may be used as either a summer or winter squash.

The novelty squash, Vegetable Spaghetti, makes a low-calorie substitute for pasta.

are planted in with the corn, making one hill of squash or pumpkin for every 6 hills of corn. After the final cultivation, the vines will quickly cover the ground beneath the corn stalks and help to control weeds. Keep the corn rows 3-1/2ft (1.5m) from each other so that sufficient sun will reach the squash. Corn yields will not be significantly affected, unless it's an extremely dry year.

All squashes have both a surface network of roots and some deep ones. In fertile soils, well supplied with humus, the roots can eventually penetrate to a depth of 3ft (90cm) or more. This means that once a week you should apply enough water to reach these roots. To do so, make a circular furrow 4in (10cm) deep around the outer spread of the root network. Allow the hose to trickle water into the furrow for at least an hour. Sufficient water is extremely important with squash because the huge leaves give off large quantities of moisture. This process is called transpiration and is necessary for cooling the plants. Watering should begin around the middle of June.

The most effective way to control weeds in a squash patch is to use a Dutch hoe or to pull them by hand. As for insects, using aluminum foil or aluminized construction paper as a mulch will repel some of the troublesome pests, eliminate the direct damage caused by feeding insects, and reduce the chance of viral diseases being transmitted to the squash.

Gourmet Summer Squash

- **Gold Rush Hybrid** — An All-American winner, this zucchini was bred especially for gardens with limited space.
- **Burpee Golden Zucchini** — A unique, golden squash with a delicious and distinctive flavor.

- **Artistocrat Hybrid** — This bushy plant won an AAS award for its very high eating quality. The rounded fruits are relatively slow growers.
- **Early Golden Summer Crookneck** — This popular variety has a superior flavor, fine texture and is very good for freezing.
- **Kuta Hybrid** — The sweet, nutty taste of this squash is a gourmet's delight. The plants can be eaten when small, like zucchini, or allowed to reach maturity for baking and storage.
- **White Bush Hybrid** — This F1 hybrid is an improved version of the English marrow. While the eating quality is good when the fruits are large, for superlative gourmet quality use them when they reach a length of 6 to 8in (15 to 20cm).
- **Peter Pan Hybrid** — This brand new scallop squash has recently been awarded the AAS bronze medal. Vigorous bushes produce early fruits to be eaten young, but even larger fruits will remain tender, unlike normal scallop squash.

Gourmet Winter Squash
- **Jersey Golden Acorn** — A new, bush-form plant that may be used as either summer or winter squash and will fit into the small garden where regular vining winter squash would not.
- **Early Butternut** — This F1 hybrid and AAS winner has brought valuable new features to the popular butternut squash. The vines are more compact, the fruits mature 10 days earlier and they'll store well for months without losing their high eating quality.
- **Table King Acorn** — An excellent keeper, this squash won an AAS silver medal for all-round superior quality.
- **Blue Hubbard** — A thick-fleshed, high yielding strain whose fruits grow to an enormous size, averaging 15lbs (6.8kg).
- **Gold Nugget** — The ideal bush-type squash for the small garden, this AAS winner produces tasty, turban-shaped fruits for baking.
- **Vegetable Spaghetti** — Until recently, this novelty squash was relatively unknown but is now becoming quite popular. When boiled whole for 30 minutes, the spaghetti-like contents can be scooped out and served like pasta, with tomato sauce or with butter and seasonings. Cold, it can be made into a salad. Younger fruits may be used like summer squash or prepared like eggplant. Mature vegetable spaghetti can be stored into late fall, retaining its excellent flavor, or it can be cooked and frozen. Don't compact the squash when freezing or you'll lose the spaghetti texture.

Swiss Chard

One of my favorite greens is Swiss chard. While it might not be apparent, Swiss chard is a member of the beet family. Its tangy, crumpled leaves are cooked in the same way as spinach, and the stalks may be prepared separately like asparagus. You'll also find that Swiss chard is just about the easiest vegetable to freeze. It's an excellent source of vitamins A and C and is rich in iron.

Swiss chard is extremely easy to grow. It can withstand both hot and cold temperatures and, if kept cut, will produce tender young leaves from late June until the hard frosts of autumn. The plants will live over the winter to provide delectable greens early in the following spring.

Preparation, Planting and Care

Swiss chard is not a bit choosy about the soil in which it grows, but you'll ensure the best results by digging a quantity of humus and a complete garden fertilizer into the earth before planting. Use the same amount and kind of humus and fertilizer as you would for beets, carrots or beans. The seeds can go into the ground as soon as it becomes workable and they should be sown 1/2in (1cm) deep. When the new plants are 8in (20cm) high, thin them to 8in (20cm) apart and cook those you have removed.

In cooler areas, a coldframe or season extender will permit sowing 3 to 4 weeks earlier than usual. Put the coldframe in place and use a heat lamp for a week to allow the earth to warm up sufficiently to permit digging, raking and sowing. You can also lengthen the season by sowing some seeds in 3in (7.5cm) pots in mid-April. The seedlings may be moved to the garden around the middle of May in most areas. Where the earth and air temperatures remain cool until early June, sow the seeds indoors in mid-May. Thirty plants will provide 10ft (3m) outdoors. You can have succulent leaves for an additional 6 weeks at the end of the season by placing the same coldframe over part of the row in early October.

When it comes time to harvest, pick the outer leaves or cut off the entire plant 2 to 3in (5 to 7.5cm) above the crown and a new crop of leaves will soon replace them. Keep in mind that leaves should be picked as they reach maturity. If you can't use them, freeze the excess

Rhubard Swiss Chard and Fordhook Giant Swiss Chard.

rather than allowing the leaves to become overripe. Older leaves will develop an earthy taste which many people find objectionable. The ideal time for cooking the leaves is when they're 6 to 10in (15 to 25cm) long.

Gourmet Swiss Chard

- **Burgundy/Rhubarb** — One of the best varieties, superior in eating quality and tempting in appearance. It makes a colorful addition to the flower border or a table arrangement.
- **Fordhook Giant/Lucullus** — The most popular green Swiss chard, the fleshy leaves make tender greens and the pearly white stalks are excellent when cooked like asparagus.

Tomatoes

In 1981, 50 million North Americans were growing their own vegetables and their favorite was tomatoes. In the past year, hundreds of thousands of tons were produced in home gardens so it hardly seems possible that 350 years ago the English regarded tomatoes as poisonous. The "love apple", as it was called, was brought to England from South America and grown only as an ornamental plant. It's really a tropical herb related to the eggplant, pepper and potato, and is a "kissing cousin" to the deadly nightshade.

There's almost always room for a few tomato plants in the garden, but someone with a very small plot may be wary of such vigorous plants. If this is the case, 5 or 6 plants staked and positioned at the back of the flower border won't look a bit out of place and will produce a plentiful supply of fruits for eating fresh, preserving or freezing.

Anyone with a sunny balcony or patio can easily grow tomatoes in containers which are at least 12in (30cm) in width and depth. Indoors, with a sunny window or special lighting, you can grow the small-fruited, miniature tomatoes like Tumblin Tom, Small Fry or Toy Boy. Toy Boy is an excellent variety to grow in hanging baskets.

Preparation, Planting and Care

The best way to grow tomatoes is to start the seeds indoors in peat-fibre pots, sowing 3 seeds to each container. When the seedlings reach 2in (5cm) in height, thin to the strongest plant per pot. Maintain the temperature at 70-75°F (21-24°C) during the germination period which will be anywhere from 5 to 8 days. Around the middle of May, on sunny days when the air temperature is above 60°F (16°C), the plants should be moved outdoors and brought back in at night. This will harden them off so that there won't be any set-back when the tomatoes are finally placed outdoors permanently.

Ten years of research at Cornell University clearly indicate that young tomato seedlings have consistently performed better than older transplants. From plant to plant, variety to variety, growth and yields have been more uniform and predictable. The ideal plant is 7in (17.5cm) tall and has 5 to 7 leaves. In all probability, you'll have trouble obtaining plants of this size from commercial growers who respond to the demand for larger plants.

If, during a particularly warm spring, you set out very large plants bearing open flowers or small green tomatoes, the first mature fruits, though early, will often be small and poorly formed. These early tomatoes can cost you dearly, since total yields may well be severely reduced.

To obtain the earliest possible tomatoes, it's preferable to use a season extender or plastic cloche and select a quick-maturing variety such as Sub-Arctic. Set out small, vigorously growing seedlings rather than using large, older plants of a late-maturing kind. During years when the late spring temperatures are too cool and thus unfavorable to early setting of fruits, the younger, smaller plants will begin to produce as early as the larger ones.

When growing tomatoes from seed, then, keep in mind these new findings and modify your traditional planting schedule so that the plants are set outdoors about 2 or 3 weeks later than usual.

If you're growing transplants in containers, place a 2in (5cm) layer of composted cattle manure, material from the home garden compost, or spent mushroom manure on top of the drainage material in the bottom of the pot. The same types of humus should make up one-third of the soil mixture. This rule applies to soil in the garden as well.

In addition, there is a special tomato food on the market which should be added to the soil before planting, at the rate recommended by the manufacturer. Out in the garden, work the earth, fertilizer and humus together down to a depth of 8in (20cm).

Tomatoes respond particularly well to a starter solution which will lessen transplanting shock and get them off to a quick start. Commercially prepared products, very high in phosphorus, are widely available or you can make your own using one of the soluable 20-20-20 fertilizers. I recommend making a starter solution of 1T (15ml) of fertilizer per gallon (4.5L) of water. Each plant should be given a cup (227ml) of the solution at planting time.

The traditional way of growing tomatoes in the garden is to let them sprawl over the ground or to stake them. In today's smaller gardens, it's best to use stakes. Such plants will produce fruits a week to 10 days sooner and won't take up nearly as much room. Tomato plants that are to be staked can be set as close as 18in (45cm) apart in the row and the rows made 24in (60cm) apart. Staked tomatoes should be kept pruned to one stem only, and the stake must be put in place at planting time. If you wait until the plants have grown tall enough to require them before putting the stakes in place, serious damage can be done to the rather shallow root system.

Since the plants will produce about 10lbs (4.5kg) or more of fruit, don't stint on the strength of your stakes. I recommend using wood which is 1in by 1in (2.5cm by 2.5cm) and long enough to extend 6ft

(1.8m) above the ground. Place each stake close to the plant, on the west side.

As the plants grow, loop string or some other tying material loosely above each fruit cluster and then around the stake. Be sure not to make the loop too tight or the main stem of the plant may be girdled, causing it to die or, at the very least, become stunted.

In large gardens, where it's only necessary to stake a few plants to get early fruits, the tomatoes can be set 3ft (90cm) apart each way, and allowed to sprawl over the ground.

Once the plants have really started to grow vigorously, you'll notice sucker, or axil, growth forming between the main stem and the leaves. This should be promptly pinched off as soon as it becomes apparent. I strongly advise applying a mulch at this point as well, but before doing so give the plants a feeding with one of the special tomato foods and a final shallow cultivation with the Dutch hoe to work it in and to get rid of weeds.

Any of the materials used as humus before planting will make a satisfactory mulch. To be effective, it should be spread 3in (7.5cm) deep. The mulch will end the need for further cultivation, keep the roots cool during hot weather, and help preserve moisture in the soil. Quite a number of home gardeners are reporting success using black plastic as a mulch.

Every time a new cluster of blossoms appears on the plants they should be treated with a hormone spray. These sprays are readily available and their use will stop blossom-drop, encourage the flowers to set many more fruits, and will also result in earlier and better quality tomatoes. You'll probably need to do this until the end of June.

Careful and regular watering from the time the plants are first set outside is a big help in preventing blossom end rot. A lack of adequate moisture in the soil when the tomatoes are small will cause some of the cells in the newly developing fruits to collapse and die. As the tomato grows, the area of dead tissue swells with it and results in the ugly black patches at its base which many home gardeners blame on disease. It's vital, then, to give the plants a good soaking once a week from planting time until harvest. Leave the sprinkler in one place long enough for the water to penetrate the soil to 6in (15cm). A 3in (7.5cm) mulch, put in place towards the end of June, is also helpful in this respect.

The metal or plastic tomato cages which are now generally available offer many benefits. Their strength and rigidity provide uniform support for the young plants as they grow. If they're grown inside the cage, staking and tying will be unnecessary. Because the cages promote the growth of tall, straight plants with plenty of protective foliage, the danger of sun scalding, splitting, and ground rot is greatly reduced. The result is exceptionally high yields.

Tests on the effects of tomato cages have recorded yields of up to 200 tomatoes per plant. What's more, the cage makes a perfect frame for a "mini-greenhouse", or cloche. When plastic is placed over the frame, the plants are protected from winds and cool night air, allowing them to be set in the ground 10 days to 2 weeks early.

Plastic cages are also available where 3 or 4 plants are set in the ground around the outside of the cage. A mixture of material from the home garden compost factory and one of the special organic tomato foods is placed inside.

If you're growing tomatoes in containers, use large peat-fibre, plastic or clay pots 12in (30cm) deep and 12in (30cm) wide. You can also buy or build a wooden box measuring 16in (40cm) by 16in (40cm) by 24in (60cm) deep. Nail a 6ft (1.8m) stake at each corner of the planter.

Commercial tomato soils are available but you can make your own using 2 parts top soil to 1 part humus. To each gallon (4.5L) of the soil/humus mixture, add a small handful of one of the special tomato foods.

Plants growing in containers will probably need twice as much watering as those in the garden. They'll also require a second feeding of tomato food in late June which should be enough to last the entire season.

One of the only insects that can cause real problems for tomatoes is the cutworm. It's extremely frustrating to set out some good-looking plants and then have them cut off at the base a couple of days later by these greyish-brown or black larvae. A cardboard collar 6in (15cm) wide and 6in (15cm) deep, set half in and half out of the ground around each plant, will deter the cutworms.

Probably the ugliest insect to attack the garden is the tomato hornworm, a caterpiller with a prominent horn at its end and diagonal white bars along its sides. To eliminate them, knock the worms off the plants into a tin can containing kerosene. It's best to do this in the early morning or evening when the hornworm is active and visible on the plants.

Tomatoes can be frozen so successfully that there's really no need to can them. Select large fruits from varieties like Beefmaster, Big Boy, or Floramerica. Wash and dry them and put 6 in a plastic freezer bag. When you want to use them, remove 2 or 3 bags and while they're still frozen run them under hot water for 10 seconds. Remove the skin which will now slip off easily, take out the core, and then slice or quarter them. Use frozen tomatoes in any recipe that calls for canned tomatoes; if you allow them to thaw you'll lose all the water they contain.

You can make uncooked, frozen tomatoes into stew or juice and,

[*Above*] *The new Sub-Arctic Maxi has a remarkable ability to set fruits in cool weather.*

[*Left*] *Early Cascade Hybrid bears an average of 70 fruits per plant.*

when they're fully cooked, you can place whole tomatoes back in the freezer. They'll come out tasting almost as good as if they were garden fresh. Uncooked tomato pulp can also be frozen and stored for several months before it's used for cooking.

Gourmet Tomatoes

The home gardener can now select tomatoes that are either determinate or indeterminate. Put simply, this means that varieties which will continue to grow and bear fruit as long as the weather stays warm have an indeterminate growing period. On the other hand, the determinate types have been bred to produce all their fruit over a 4 to 5 week period. Determinate varieties are compact, making them ideal plants to grow in containers. They are also the tomatoes to choose in short-season areas, or if you just want the earliest possible crop.

By far the most tomatoes are of the indeterminate type and in the following list of recommended varieties each breed should be regarded as such unless specifically referred to as determinate.

When hybrid tomatoes were first introduced, their eating quality left much to be desired. This is no longer true. Hybrid plants are extremely vigorous, uniform, and produce large crops of high-quality fruit. Each seed of a hybrid is the result of controlled pollination, using two distinct parent lines. The results are outstanding and whenever possible the home gardener should select a hybrid variety.

- **Early Girl** — This Fl hybrid is the earliest regular-sized tomato and will produce a heavy crop for a longer period than most other early varieties. The coloring is excellent and the flavor is sweet yet slightly tart.
- **Pixie Hybrid** — A determinate tomato, ideal for growing in containers, flower borders or small gardens as well as indoors. The plants are compact and bear heavy loads of fruits with a surprising "big tomato" taste.
- **Early Cascade Hybrid** — A very early variety which prefers to be staked and pruned or grown in a special tomato cage. It's a heavy and continuous bearer, averaging as many as 70 fruits per plant.
- **Sub-Arctic** — A new family of tomatoes with astounding and unique characteristics. Extremely heavy fruiting occurs much earlier than with most tomatoes and they have a remarkable ability to set fruits in cool weather. The best of this new group of determinate tomatoes are **Sub-Arctic Maxi** and **Sub-Arctic Plenty**.
- **Sweet 100** — A unique new cherry tomato which produces amazingly high yields with staked plants carrying multiple clusters of up to 100 or more fruits each for a total yield of some 2,000 tomatoes per plant! It's an early bearer and continues to produce heavily until the first frost.
- **Long Keeper** — This winter storage tomato may be gathered ripe, or partially ripe, before frost. Stored correctly, it will stay fresh for 6 to 12 weeks. Although the taste and texture can't compare with fruits picked fresh, Long Keeper is superior to the expensive tomatoes you'll find in the stores in mid-winter.
- **Delicious** — Tomatoes produced by this variety usually weigh well over a pound (450g), have excellent flavor and smoothness and very little cracking. The world's largest recorded tomato was a whopping 6lb-8oz (3kg) Delicious.

Turnips

Summer Turnips

People who have never tried the white summer turnips are always amazed at their eating quality. They're a cool weather crop grown for eating in early summer and again in the fall. They can be eaten when the turnips are 2in (5cm) across, about 35 days after seeding.

Summer turnips have long been a tremendous favorite with the Japanese. They have contributed **Tokyo Cross** to our gardens, an All-America winner that has proven to be the finest of all the summer turnips. At maturity, it measures 6in (15cm) across without being pithy or losing its perfect shape. No other kind can touch Tokyo Cross for flavor, quality and tenderness. I find it also stays fresh for a very long time after the roots are ready for harvesting. It can be peeled and cooked in the same way as potatoes or rutabagas, served with salt, pepper and butter. When it's very young, it can be eaten raw like radishes.

I'd suggest making two sowings, one just as soon as the earth becomes workable in the spring and another as late as August 1, for harvesting in October. If space in your garden is limited, the seeds for the last sowing can be broadcast between the rows of corn. Prepare the soil for planting with humus and a complete garden fertilizer and sow the seed 1/2in (1cm) deep in rows 15in (40cm) apart. When the young turnip plants are 2in (5cm) high, thin them to 4in (10cm) apart. The tops of the various kinds of summer turnips all make excellent greens. The **Just Right Hybrid** will give you heavy, fine flavored tops, loaded with vitamins A and C, one month after seeding. You'll need 4ft (120cm) of row for every person you plan to feed, and another 10ft (3m) for the second sowing. One package will seed 30ft (9m) of row, so two packages should be enough for the average family of four.

Rutabagas/Swede Turnips

Many people are put off by the large size and rather coarse appearance of rutabagas before they can enjoy their delightful, spicy flavor. These yellow, winter turnips are extremely easy to grow and provide inexpensive, healthful and hearty eating throughout the fall and winter.

To ensure a heavy crop, prepare the soil with plenty of humus and a complete garden fertilizer as you would for carrots or beets. Sow the

The finest of all summer turnips is Tokyo Cross

seed during the last 2 weeks of June, laying them 1/2in (1cm) deep and covering them with fine soil. When the young seedlings are 3in (7.5cm) high thin to 6in (15cm) apart.

American, Laurentian, or **American Purple Top** as it's variously called, is the best yellow-fleshed variety. Its large roots are purple above the ground and light yellow below. Ninety days after sowing you can start eating them raw or cooked.

Many home gardeners tell me that **Macomber,** a sweet, white-fleshed rutabaga, is more delicious than American Purple Top. Its flesh is white and fine-grained and the flavor is surprisingly sweet and mild. The roots are white with purplish-green shoulders. Large, smooth and round, they have practically no neck.

Both the yellow and white-fleshed rutabagas will keep well all winter when waxed, stored in the cellar in moist sand, or buried deep in a pit outdoors.

Herbs

An herb garden can be a very rewarding project, particularly if you enjoy cooking. Even though herbs have come to us from all over the world, most of them have easily adapted to the North American garden. They will grow well in any soil that's suitable for vegetables and, while they prefer full sun, herbs will do much better than most garden plants in partially shaded spots. What's more, herbs produce attractive flowers and foliage which can be a beautiful addition to a flower bed, foundation planting, rock garden, or decorative container where they receive a minimum of 4 hours of sunlight a day. Given the right conditions, many herbs can even be grown indoors.

Preparation, Planting and Care

In preparing the soil for an outdoor herb garden, add a large quantity of humus and a complete garden fertilizer, such as a 5-10-5 or a 4-12-8, to the earth. Scatter the fertilizer at a rate of 1/2lb (224g) for each 9sq ft (.8sq m) of garden area. On top of this , apply humus at the rate of 1 bushel (35L) for the same area. The best forms of humus for herbs are composted cattle manure, material from the compost factory, discarded mushroom manure, or peat moss. Rake 2 or 3 times to level and remove any debris.

Where a few plants are added to a flower bed or some other part of the garden, make the earth one-third humus and add a small handful of fertilizer in the spot you will be planting. As with the larger herb garden, the earth, humus and fertilizer should be mixed together down to a depth of 8in (20cm) before putting the plants in the ground.

For growing herbs in containers, use a mixture of 2 parts top soil, 1 part humus, and 1 part coarse horticultural or builder's sand. To every bushel (35L), add 1/2lb (224g) of a complete garden fertilizer. Half of a large barrel, such as those used by distilleries, makes an ideal planter for herbs.

Seeds or started plants can be obtained from all the usual gardening sources. If started plants are set out in mid-May or a little later, they will still be green and supplying fresh leaves until late September or on into November, depending on your climate. You can remove 2 hard cuttings from the plants in August or early September for drying and you'll still have a good fresh supply for use in the autumn.

The same care should be given herbs as for most vegetables. Sprinkle them thoroughly once a week, allowing the water to penetrate 5 to 6in (12.5 to 15cm) into the soil. Herbs should be side-dressed with a complete garden fertilizer the first week in July and again in August if you've made cuttings.

Anyone who hasn't grown herbs before would be advised to start out with half a dozen of the easiest varieties to handle. I'd suggest sweet basil, sage, mint, parsley, summer savory, and thyme.

Herbs growing indoors require the same conditions as the majority of houseplants. That is, plenty of sun or special artificial lighting, adequate moisture in the air, and night temperatures dropping to about 60°F (16°C).

Chives, mint, thyme, sage, parsley, marjoram, sweet basil and quite a few other annual, biennial and perennial herbs are easy to grow indoors and make quite handsome potted plants as well. As mentioned before, you'll need a sunny window or special plant lights, or you could set up a simple apartment/basement greenhouse.

The indoor greenhouse requires little or no structure. Simply suspend 2 or 3 of the 40 watt daylight, fluorescent tubes over a table. If you're growing from seed, the tube should be 6in (15cm) above the table until germination occurs, and then raised to 12in (30cm).

One of the main problems to overcome indoors is a lack of sufficient moisture in the air. I'd recommend buying a small plastic tray, 6 to 8in (15 to 20cm) wide, and deep enough to hold a minimum of 2in (5cm) of pebbles. It should be long enough to fit the window sill or the fluorescent light set-up in your "greenhouse". Add water to the tray and maintain the level at 1/2in (1cm) below the bottom of the pots at all times. Using a portable humidifier is the best guarantee of keeping the humidity reading at a level sufficient for growing healthy plants.

You can also cut down on moisture loss by enclosing your fluorescent lights and plant trays in a plastic "tent". If your lights are on a timer, the covered unit may be left for a week or more without any attention. The moisture from the trays will condense on the surface of the plastic and fall back onto the plants, meaning that additional water is required much less frequently.

If the herbs are growing in an adequate soil mixture and there's sufficient moisture in the air, they'll only need one good soaking a week with room temperature water. During the months of May, June, July and August, though, you'll probably need to water plants that are in full sun twice a week. If you must use hard, chlorinated tap water, let it stand overnight before watering. Mist the leaves and stems daily with lukewarm water to help unclog the plant pores and maintain their health and vigor.

Use a soluable or liquid indoor plant food once a month and be sure not to use more than the recommended amount. It's always better to underfeed than to overfeed.

Harvesting, Drying and Storage

Fresh green leaves can be picked from the majority of herbs and used for cooking just as soon as they are produced. Where you have only 2 or 3 plants, however, you may wish to wait until the plants are larger and growing more vigorously before making cuttings.

August is the time to start picking the foliage of most garden-grown herbs for drying. The common practice of trying to salvage a few tough, old plants at this time for repotting indoors is seldom satisfactory. The best way to have an indoor winter herb garden is to start new plants from seed at the beginning of August, using 5 or 6in (12.5 to 15cm) containers. If kept in active growth, these plants should produce usable foliage all winter long. They probably won't bloom indoors, so you won't get the seeds from such plants as dill or coriander, but I prefer their leaves to the more pungent seeds anyway.

The best time to pick leaves for drying and storing is in the morning, after the dew has dried. Don't expose the leaves to sun after they've been picked because the volatile oils which give them their flavor will evaporate. Herbs should be picked, tied in a bunch, moved immediately to a dark attic or well-ventilated cupboard, and hung upside down. Some herbs will dry faster than others, but you'll know when they're ready for storage when the leaves become brittle and make a noise when touched. Don't allow them to become so dry that they turn to dust. All herbs should be stored in air-tight containers in a dark place for best results.

Gourmet Herbs

Chives

One of the best herbs for growing in the garden or indoors is chives. In the garden, sow the seed rather thickly over the surface and don't cover them with soil. Older plants may be divided and repotted, but be sure to separate them into several individual segments rather than replanting as one solid clump.

Mint

Numerous varieties of mint can be grown by the home gardener, but I suggest starting with spearmint or apple mint. Most varieties are difficult to grow from seed, so the best method is to put rooted plants out in the spring. Since these plants are so vigorous, I prefer to use large containers rather than having them overrun the rest of the garden. For the same reason, you'll have to replace the old plants every 3 years with young shoots. Ideally, mint should be harvested before it

Peppermint

Sage

Chives

blooms, usually in June or July, because the oil content will then be at its highest.

Parsley

Because parsley takes so long to germinate (3 to 4 weeks), it's best to start seeds indoors. If you do start them outside, soak the seeds

Sweet Basil

Thyme

Extra Curled Dwarf Parsley

W. ATLEE BURPEE CO.

overnight and then wash them with warm water before sowing. I often mix the parsley seed with some fast-maturing radish seed which will mark the rows. The curly parsley may be gathered any time from mid-June until mid-September but the attractive color and distinctive flavor will only be retained if you dry it rapidly in a very warm place. Once dry, the parsley should be rubbed from the stems and stored immediately so that the leaves will not absorb any moisture and be ruined. Freezing is another simple way to keep parsley. No blanching is required and the frozen parsley, if rubbed between your hands, will thaw looking as though it were freshly chopped.

Some outstanding varieties which I recommend are **Curlina**, for its tolerance to hot weather; **Unicurl**, for its uniquely curled leaves; and **Darki**, for its tolerance to cold weather.

Sage

Surely one of the most useful herbs that can be grown at home is sage. The best variety for most indoor and outdoor gardens is the broad-leaved type because it's so easy to dry and harvest, but all sage is simple to grow from seed. You can make sowings twice, at the beginning and the end of the normal gardening season, but you'll find that sage, being a perennial, will produce richer foliage after the first year. Once the plants are established, you can make 2 cuttings for drying purposes each season, once in June and again in August. You'll find the stems difficult to break by hand and that the rather tough leaves need to be dried longer than most other herbs.

Sweet Basil

We grow sweet basil as an annual when it is in fact a tender perennial of tropical origins. Therefore it should not be set outside until the danger of frost has passed. Either sow the seeds indoors in March, or purchase started plants in individual containers. Avoid bare-root seedlings which will not transplant well. In June or early July the plants will produce tall, flowering spikes which should be pinched off or much of the plant's energy will go into producing useless seeds. When harvesting, be extremely careful not to bruise the tender foliage of this herb and wash the leaves only if absolutely necessary. The dried leaves should be stripped off the stems before storing.

Thyme

Both the common and lemon thyme make attractive border plants or ground covers when grown outdoors. If started from seed, however, the plants won't reach a usable size for about 2 years. The plants will bloom in early June and, for drying purposes, should be harvested just before they come into flower. Shoots about 6in (15cm) long are tied together or laid on a tray to dry in a warm, dark place. When its thoroughly dry, rub the thyme through a coarse sieve and store properly.